End to Ending

an Appalachian Trail Thru-Hiker's Story

by
Tanner Critz

Temenos Publishing Company

Cover art by Tanner Critz.
Photos courtesy Tanner Critz
More can be found at www.EndtoEnding.com

ISBN 978-0-9846199-1-7

Temenos Publishing
411 Main St.
North Little Rock, AR 72114
501-772-7602
www.temenospublishing.com

For the Vikings, who are always with me.

Adventure Always!

Tammy Cravit

Waya the Wolf

You can tell a thru-hiker, also known as an end-to-ender, when you see him on the trail. Like a wild bear, he will seem powerful and wary, filthy and noble, weary but with the woods as his crutch and not his assailant. His is an experience that cannot be found through windshields or sunglasses and does not penetrate the barriers of fresh clothing and fragrance that surround us every day. It stalks him quietly as weeks and months of hiking dissolve into his bones and the fragile web of civilized pleasantry is tattered by passing branches and swarming bugs. It infects his mind as thoughts of hunger surpass those of sex, weariness, and cleanliness. It pounces one day when he no longer sees and smells and feels nature, but *is* nature, and realizes that he is surrounded by the wild and mysterious beasts who are us.

PROLOGUE

In the summer of 1976 I was three years old; my fingers spread softly over the backseat of our chewed-up silver car. The upholstery was starting to crack and my oversized head bobbed softly as we sped over the rolling, docile miles between Nashville and Memphis. I dreamed lightly out the window at the brilliant roadside trees, racing into patterns that only crayons could faithfully depict.

My parents were so young then, hardly older than I am now. My mother was wearing a homemade, tie-dyed T-shirt that swirled into an island of yellows, oranges, and reds. Her face was soft and smooth and smiling. My father's beard grew monumental and wild from his jaw and neck, nearly eclipsing his mouth. He was driving absently and debating with her. It was the kind of laughing disagreement that wasn't so much an argument as an act of intimate dispute. This one was about me.

"He thinks the world is flat," my mother said, pleading and motioning out the dusty windows. "He looks around and it looks flat and he has no reason to think it's different anywhere else!"

"Come on," my father looked at her over his glasses. "He's a lot more perceptive than that. There's a globe in the house, he knows that's the world, he hears people talking, he knows it's round without having to see the curve." They went back and forth about faith and reason for a while before my father said, "Hold on. Tanner." He leaned back over the seat and changed his voice to the soft, melodic tone that signaled me to tune in. "Do you think the world is flat?"

No," I said with certainty, looking back out the window. My father's eyes darted back to my mother, a victorious grin peeking through his great beard. I stared out the window for a moment before completing my thought. "It's bumpy."

Sixteen years later I was in a map shop in Atlanta, and I picked up a book called *The Appalachian Trail Backpacker* by Victoria and Frank Louge. I can't recall why I took notice of the book detailing equipment and preparation for hiking the 2,160-mile trail. I had never even been backpacking before. I only knew I had always loved the feel and smell of standing amongst mountains, and every page I turned in the book brought me closer to the realization that I would hike it myself.

I spent two years saving money for the equipment and food, read a little bit more, asked a little bit more, and went on an overnight hike. I told the director of my college program that I would be missing a semester and fought to be sure that nothing else in my life could be planned to intersect with that time. I tried to find a friend to go along with me, but in the end I settled for starting the trail on my own. When I found myself on the top of Springer Mountain in Georgia on March 15, 1995, the beginning of the Appalachian National Scenic Trail that follows two-by-six inch white paint blazes through Georgia, North Carolina, Tennessee, Virginia, West Virginia, Maryland, Pennsylvania, New Jersey, New York, Connecticut, Massachusetts, Vermont, New Hampshire, and Maine, before winding up to the peak of Mount Katahdin in Baxter State Park, I was birthed into a new reality.

Tanner Critz
Wayah the Wolf
Lord of the Vikings

CHAPTER 1

Wayah Bald, North Carolina
117 miles down and 2,051 miles to go

"You must leave now, take what you need, you think will last."

Bob Dylan

When I awoke March 25th, I began to notice little things that weren't quite right. My bed was harder than usual, my pillow unyielding. There was a ghostly fabric looming only a foot or so from my head. I became aware of a spoiled, oddly familiar smell hanging in the air all around me. Recognition began to seep in, and then like a spray of cold water, understanding. I was in my tent, not my bed. I was in the woods, not my house. This was to be my tenth day hiking the Appalachian Trail, and my fifth day of being alone.

I stared at the roof of the cocoon-like tent for a while, watching sunlight patterning on the thin, stretched nylon. The mountain dawn was a bright, crisp white, since the sun had been rising a while before it came over the ridge. I could hear the chatty spring a few yards away and listened to the loud absence of walls around me. During the night my heavy bones had slowly settled into each other and forgotten where they began and ended. I soaked up the syrupy warmth of my sleeping bag like a chrysalis and tasted the cooler, wetter air of the tent on my face. When I moved, I did so carefully, mindful of my weary feet and legs and back. I was growing used to the fact that, though I ached to the point of stinging before going to bed, the night would leave only soreness in its wake, and most of that was dampened within the first hour of walking. Nevertheless, I always wondered if my body would eventually wear down and break, and I tried to imagine how I would be able to tell that pain from the daily aches that came with eight or nine hours of carrying my hefty pack through the mountains.

Three years earlier I had been hospitalized when an ulcer in my stomach had bled me nearly to death. At the time I hadn't been able to distinguish that pain from the dull ache in my abdomen after hours of karate and kickboxing each day. I had let it go for a long time, blaming each symptom on being kicked in the belly, having the flu, and so on, until I collapsed during a tournament from anemia. After several transfusions and conversations with confused doctors for whom I was far from the profile for such an ailment, I was released and deemed recovered. Two years later it happened again. At the time I was in the process of planning my thru-hike and there was a good deal of concern from doctors and parents over what would happen if I started bleeding again in the woods. After the second episode a theory was being kicked around the medical community about my ulcers being the result of a bacterial infection instead of stress and eating habits, as I was a very relaxed and fit teenager. Since I was determined to hike anyway, I was given a vial of prescription acid-inhibitors and a vial of antibiotics to carry with me in case I had an episode in the woods.

Despite the pains and the growing loneliness, or maybe because of them, I felt centered. On what, was harder to say. Through the aching, the climbing, the dirtiness and the quiet, an air of pleasurable weariness hung around my head that made me very comfortable in the base motions and movements of the hike, the camp, and the cook-fire. Katahdin was so far away that to think of it as a goal made me feel very small and lonely, so I focused more tightly: getting up, breaking camp, walking a few miles.

My sleeping bag and its warmth came off reluctantly, but once out of it, I wasted no time in leaving the tent. The little one-and-a-half-man tent was too small for me to even sit up straight in and barely afforded room to get into my shorts and heavy fleece pullover. I crunched my knees to my chest, turned my feet to the door, and unzipped the mesh entrance. My big, black boots wouldn't fit entirely under the tiny vestibule of the tent, but the toes could hang out under the flap and still resist any rain that might come along. Where they had been exposed to the night air beads of moisture clung to the leather, reminding me of how new they were. Before the Trail I had only hiked twenty-two miles in them. One overnight hike. Of course the same was true for the rest of my gear, and me for that matter. Even so, my feet slid easily into the boots and dropped into the snug socket around the heel. I laced them up soundly but lightly, not wanting to cramp the flow of blood through my ankles as my feet swelled later in the day. I felt solid and steady in the mountain boots. They still smelled like leather, and once I laced them up they pleasantly intercepted the reek from my socks. I had three pairs, but three days of constant hiking in each pair had left them all pretty ripe. A few days earlier I had tried to wash them with liquid soap on a frosty afternoon in a high mountain stream. The icy water that sloshed over my already cold hands made them numb almost instantly, and as I hastily scrubbed the socks, dipping them now and again to try to get the suds off, the numbness evolved into a hard, crushing ache. Before I was halfway finished I threw the sudsy, wet socks across a rail, rammed my hands into my fleece and curled my body around them to fight back the feeling that my hands were lost for good. When in the morning the socks were solid with ice, I was further fortified in my decision that the stink was a better friend than the cold and let the socks smell how they wanted

5

after that, planning to wash them in the distant warmth of summer.

I brushed some of the dirt and moisture off the inside of the rainfly that covered my tent's vestibule and pushed past it into the frigid mountain air. Climbing out of the tent is one of the great rewards of camping. It's like being born every morning. The warm, soft, musky shell with all its layers is pulled off, and you stretch out to more than twice its height, reaching your arms to the trees and letting every joint, tendon, and muscle unwind to its fullest. You let your bones separate and the crystal talons of the morning air invade your pores as you breathe in the pure, high mountain air and realize that the whole world starts beneath your feet and extends down and away forever. For that moment before you breathe out, you, too, extend through the brook and the earth and the trail, beyond the trees and the horizon and the sky. For that moment you have no bounds and no limits, and there's nothing you cannot do.

Slightly less glamorous is the next part of the morning, when the countdown begins for you to find a suitable spot to dig a toilet hole. It was not an uncommon decision on cold nights for me to ignore the body's functions in favor of uninterrupted warmth, leading to a fairly dynamic morning rush. After filling in my ditch and putting away my trowel, I settled down on a log near a blackened old fire pit and cooked up a small pot of water on my little camp stove for tea and oatmeal. The oatmeal was routine by this time, but the tea was a new experiment on the trail. I felt very cosmopolitan with the tag hanging out of my flimsy plastic cup, and the hot tea nestled very comfortably between my chilly hands. I thought I must have looked like a picture in one of those camping magazines, except dirtier and with no hair. I felt the steam flow past my face as I looked out off Wine Spring Mountain. I had made my camp at the very top of the small, winter-stripped mountain, and the view into the valleys beyond was mostly cluttered by the gray-brown skeletons of trees and the arching green boughs of rhododendron around the spring. It hadn't taken long to get used to staring past those gray, southern trees and to wonder where among the valleys and hills the Trail would lead each day. My body was almost getting used to the abuse of hiking with the sixty-pound pack all day, and though climbing mountains would never become really easy, I was beginning to feel the world around me instead of only feeling my legs and feet and shoulders and the pounding of my heart.

I had been hiking alone for five days and hadn't seen a soul for three. I crossed into North Carolina from Georgia with Bob the Postman, but he had gotten ahead of me that day, and I never saw him again. Even though I grew up as an only child with both parents working, I was used to having people around for some part of the day. The solitude was beginning to reach me on a very personal level. The laughter, posturing, aches, and general camaraderie of the hikers I had met during the first few days had been a welcome distraction. It felt like we were all in the classroom without a teacher, and no one knew quite how to act. We just watched each other having our personal problems with feet and gear and attitude and wondered quietly who would make it all the way and who would limp off to town at the next road crossing. One man hurt his knee the first day and decided to stay behind in the shelter the next. One woman was starting to lose toenails the third day. One girl had a dog who wasn't adjusting well to the chaffing from its little dog-pack. Our packs were heavy, our days were hard, and the task ahead was Olympian. I had virtually no idea what I was doing. I spent a lot of time watching other hikers and trying to pick up useful tips from them, but the experience seemed to have even the two Eagle Scouts among us at the end of their wits. While they knew some tricks about how to use their packs and looked comfortable with their tents, they weren't used to the effort and the isolation.

On the second day I lost most of my nylon cord while trying to hang my food out of reach of bears as I had seen in drawings. The knotted system of branches and cord that I improvised proved to be not only bear-proof, but hiker proof, and I spent the first part of the morning jumping in the air with my knife and whacking at the only part of the cord that was in reach where I had tethered it around a tree trunk. As far as I know, the rest of that cord is still up there, prompting hikers to wonder what alien intelligence managed to bind two trees together at such a height.

There was one guy who was pretty relaxed about the whole thing. His trail name was Sir Renity, and I met him on the way up Springer Mountain the first day. Most everyone I met already had a trail name they had chosen before starting. I had read about these names that hikers go by on the trail, but hadn't thought of anything fitting for myself. Trail names were easier to remember than people's real names, and often had some sort of story behind them that said something about the hiker. Sir Renity ate fancy food and carried fresh eggs and all sorts of cooking toys with him. I would often pass him during the day, napping on a hillside or reading by a cliff. I suppose I was too caught up in trying to hike at the time to notice that he was having a bit more fun than the rest of us in spite of his heavy pack and blisters. Five days ago he had hitched off the trail to a hostel with everyone else I had met to re-supply and do some laundry. In my planning I had worked from the data book to set my re-supply points based on the miles in between them and the distance off the trail that I would have to hike or hitch to get to them. It turned out that many of the best hiker services like the hostel my companions had all known about were mentioned only in the *Thru-Hiker's Handbook,* which I had somehow managed not to include in my preparations. I had sent my mail drop based on mileage alone to the post office in Franklin, North Carolina, a couple of days farther on than the hostel, and had to keep moving on alone in order to make it there before I ran out of food.

I hadn't anticipated the impact of five days of complete solitude. Normally to achieve such a level of isolation, one must be stranded on an island or locked in solitary confinement. Not only were there no people, there was no contact with society at all. No television, Internet, phone, music, or books. I had charts and maps, read the occasional sign or mile-marker. It was surprising how quickly the loneliness turned to resigned singularity and how quickly the dialogue with myself became an elusive give-and-take instead of a series of one-sided pleas and reminders.

I was hiking longer days than most so I could catch up to the schedule I had set for my own re-supply points and not run out of food in between them. Since the boxes of food arrived at certain towns on particular days, it seemed like a tempo that couldn't be interrupted. I had estimated the distances from the comfort of my mother's living room, poring over maps and the data book in an attempt to chart twelve to fifteen miles a day, but take into account steep climbs and the locations of shelters. It had all been very academic then, but now some of those days were hard to live up to, and I was a little behind. Sitting on a log holding an empty teacup wasn't getting me there any faster, either. I needed to start breaking camp and get my body moving.

I suddenly realized that a used tea bag weighs a great deal more than a new one and, if deposited in my zip-lock trash bag with my regular trash, would make quite a mess once I crammed it into my tightly packed gear. I pulled the dripping, mottled sack out of my cup and hobbled over to the fire pit to deposit it under the half-burnt logs where it could be consumed in the next fire. My idea no longer seemed clever when I found dozens of bits of food and trash strewn through the pit. Thinking perhaps to squeeze the juice out of the bag so it would be lighter and less messy, I placed it on a large rock by the pit and used another rock to flatten it. When I opened the press, though, I found the tea bag had been reduced to a wet, flattened, torn mess of herbs and paper marinated in an inky, brown juice. I hesitantly picked up the now very light and empty paper tatters by the string and placed them in my trash bag, kicking the mess of herbs into the dirt. I pulled my green cap out of my pack and secured it to the oily, two-week-old stubble on my head. I had shaved my head a few days before starting, and now my big, pale scalp would grab on to any fabric that passed near it. I had never been bald before, but it seemed somehow fitting, and I had done it myself with an electric beard trimmer one night during a moment of courageous romanticism. The trimmer wasn't hefty like clippers, and a courageous moment turned into hours of etching my thick hairline slowly backwards, a gesture transformed into a long meditation.

I was already used to my gear, and packing it up went rather quickly: break down bedding and tent, secure on pack after shaking out and brushing off dirt and moisture, and put in their respective sacks. Arrange the stove, pots, and food in the main pouch and I was ready. I pushed aside my journal and pulled out the maps and my data book. I already knew I was seven miles behind schedule. The night before I had decided that I needed to stop at the spring on top of Wine Spring Mountain because there was no way I was going to make it to the shelter that day. To catch up to my schedule I would have to do nineteen miles to Wesser, North Carolina, a little rafting outpost by a state road. There was supposed to be a restaurant and bunks there. I unfolded the map and followed the zigzagging line of the profile display to find where I was. I rarely even looked at the directional map. All that mattered were the changes in altitude. The up and down didn't look so bad, but nineteen miles would be daunting even if it was flat. I had done nineteen six days ago when I hiked with Bob the Postman and it had damn near killed me.

The trail in Georgia had only been a seventy-five-mile chunk. On the sixth day it had felt good to cross the state line into North Carolina, marked by a pipe nailed to a tree with "GA - NC" painted on it. Now in the second state on the trail, it would be hundreds of miles before I would cross another such line. The goals I set for myself would have to be daily ones, and nineteen miles wasn't so unreasonable, especially if I could buy a hot meal that was anything other than macaroni and cheese and Ramen noodles at the end of it. The only way to know for sure was to start walking. I put away my maps, filtered some more water for the day ahead, and took off my warm fleece pullover to pack it away. It was cold on the mountaintop but being cold was motivation to start hiking and warm up. I felt strangely at home with the chill, and hefted the cold pack on my back, the pads still damp from yesterday's sweat. As I tightened the hip belt, the weight stood up obediently on my back and seemed to disappear into my own for a moment. Leaning our combined weight forward I started down the trail, pushing away a rhododendron branch weighed down by the morning dew.

Among the many benefits of sleeping on top of a mountain is beginning the day with a nice, cool downhill to get the blood flowing. A tough uphill at the wrong time could put a stop to all productive thought, but an easy morning stroll into a sleepy, mist-laced valley always got my mind working. In the five days I had been alone, I had plenty of time to think. A few days earlier I tried to think of every house I'd lived in, then everyone I had ever known, and since that only took a couple of hours I went on to try to remember everything that had ever happened to me. Over the long hours of climbing I had struggled for productive thought, tried to look over my life clearly, discover something new, remember something lost. There were many subtle implications before setting out that I should discover the meaning of life on such a journey, and I was doing my best, but my thoughts were running thin, and most of the time I was just tracking the pulse of my own consciousness. At twenty years old, I could only reflect for so long before redundancy set in, so when I could spare the breath, I would sing as I walked. It made me appreciate long songs and their ability to make miles disappear. That morning I decided to sing "A Hard Rain's Gonna Fall" as it would carry me quite a ways.

I was following the trail along the shaded side of a ridge with the moist, leaf-covered ground rising to my right and a valley dropping away to my left. The shadow of the ridge made a dark crescent in the valley, and the gentle mist clung to the shelter of the receding shade.

Where have you been, my blue-eyed son? Where have you been my darling young one? I've stumbled on the side of twelve misty mountains. I paused for a moment, wondering if I had subconsciously chosen the song because of the fitting lyrics. *I've stepped in the middle of seven sad forests.* I continued walking through the winter-stripped trees, and singing on I began to examine the lines of the traveling song more closely. I began to see more and more in the verses of the poem and, with the repeated reflection of my life fresh on my mind, began to make connections. The people and places and moments of my life rolled through my mind with the words, and I stitched each note into my life's fabric. Even where a line seemed at first to have no connection to me, the fast spinning loom found a fit and wove it in. I began to trail my life behind me like a long quilt of images and feelings as I sang. Instead of a thought coming to mind and then passing away, the heavy fabric held them all at once to be seen in a single observation, and the weight of it pulled at my neck, growing as I continued.

I've been ten thousand miles in the mouth of a graveyard. The words came slower and slower as at each new verse my mind was filled with the forces that had moved my life for better and for worse. The words of the song went on alone, measuring themselves with the falling of my feet as my mind began to race faster and faster, my thoughts overlapping and threatening collapse. *I saw a newborn baby with wild wolves all around it...I saw guns and sharp swords in the hands of young children...I heard the sound of a thunder and it roared out a warning...I heard one hundred drummers whose hands were a blazin'... I heard the sound of a clown who cried in the alley...I met a young girl and she gave me a rainbow...Oh and what'll you do now my blue-eyed son? What'll you do now my darling young one?* Breathing out sharply as my eyes teared up, I became aware that I had stopped on the trail and goosebumps rose all over my body as the forest fell silent, awaiting reply. The pulling tapestry of my life snapped free and fell gently into the leaves. I turned to look out into the valley and smelled the richness of the earth, the dying, dry chill of winter trying to hold on while deep in the valley was a sparkle of green so bright that its light was the cry of a newborn child and below it, running away into valleys beyond, was a brilliant spring throwing light into the dark woods as it ran. For a moment I could see it wandering far down the valleys, meeting other streams and creeks, growing and changing, becoming greater and faster until it spilled into the ocean, and the whole world lay out in front of me. A cold breeze blew up from the valley and brought me back, and I turned and hiked lightly along the trail.

I had reached the end of the valley and now looked up at the mountain ahead, walking steadily to meet it. The uphill was strangely welcome, each step pulling me higher and higher. Questions shot clearly into my mind as if I were climbing up into them. The questions were big, and they washed over me and through me and away. *Why am I alive? What is power? What is love? What will I do with my life?* I stepped through them like layers of mist, and when I had risen above them, they were gone. They lay in the roots and rocks by the trail for people to see and wonder who had discarded them. *Who am I? What am I doing here?* I broke out of the trees into a wide clearing with a strange tower. It seemed very out of place and I approached it with some caution. Beside the tower, a sign explained the history of this mountain named Wayah Bald. *Wayah* was the Cherokee word for the wolf spirit, a symbol of great power and strength. The mountain was the ancestral home of the wolves in Cherokee legend, but the wolves had been driven out and killed long ago. The stone tower sat on top of the bald like a mushroom with a staircase on one side, and I wound my way up to the stone cap where the view stretched all around. The world faded off to its lacy cusps, and I was entirely at peace. I shrugged off the pack and felt the cool wind catch the sweaty middle of my back as I leaned my pack against the short guard wall that encircled the rim. Opening the zipper, I pulled some nuts and granola out of the bag of snacks that was positioned closest to the top of the main pouch. Sitting on the cobbled stone wall, there was nothing in the world but the wind, the tapestry of North Carolina, and the tiny bits of granola and nuts crunching lightly in my mouth.

Something new and strange appeared below. I could see two figures making their way quickly up another path, a concrete walkway from a community parking lot. One was a short, plump woman with a camera and wide, black sunglasses. The other was a tall man who pulled his windbreaker tightly over his shoulders and looked at the ground. Gradually I could hear the woman saying, "There it is! It's not much farther now!" She was looking straight ahead at the tower, glancing down now and then at the path. Words flowed from her in an endless stream punctuated only by bursts of exclamatory laughter that did nothing to break the tempo of her speech. The man was perfectly quiet and never looked up.

"Anyway, I read in this magazine that they were gonna start puttin' wolves back in the woods, and I said to Murray that he'd better... Hey! There's somebody up on the tower already!" Her words gave way for a moment to a heavy, panting grin.

"Already?" the tall man glanced at his watch as she led him up the steps.

"Howdy!" said the woman, her cheeks red and her movements quick. She introduced herself and the man but I didn't listen to their names as they flew by. "Who are you?" She asked. The question seemed to echo around the tower and over the mountaintop. I looked back to the quiet woods where I had left the question in the rocks where the trail broke from the trees and it peeked out at me again. I turned back to the pair and found them unmoving for the first time, waiting uncomfortably for my answer.

"I'm... Wayah," I said, looking her complacently in the glasses.

"Oh?" she chuckled. "Are you from around here?" She seemed amused.

"Yes," I said thoughtfully.

"So are we! We're from Haysville. This is my brother. He sells insurance. How 'bout you?"

"I'm hiking the Appalachian Trail."

"Oh, really?" She looked at the tall man and crooked her brow. The man shrugged. "Don't you remember? That's that trail Muriel likes to hike. Goes clear to Wesser."

"Where's that?" said the tall man.

"It's that rafting place on Highway Nineteen. Oh look, it's almost eight. We'd better get moving." She shuffled back to the stairs, breathing sharply a few times and peering through her thick sunglasses. "You sure can see a lot today. Have a good one." She began to drop down the steps and the tall man nodded, following her.

I watched them go striding down the path as fast as I'd seen anyone move in ten days. "Thanks," I said quietly, nodding and smiling as they disappeared down the concrete walkway. My body felt like a leaf on the wind and I squinted into the sunlight smiling, suddenly feeling out of place on the tower. I was ready to move, and I packed my granola away and hefted the pack back onto my shoulders and hips. Strolling down the steps I said to myself, "I am Wayah, the Wolf. I'm hiking the Appalachian Trail from Georgia to Maine." I thought of the southern terminus marker on Springer Mountain in Georgia, only ten days past, and of the northern

15

terminus marker on Mount Katahdin in Maine, veiled in the tint of old photographs and the cold uncertainty of the months ahead. I looked at the two-by-six inch white blaze on the tree next to where the trail dove back into the woods and walked on down the path, gently touching the blaze as I passed and dreaming of my dinner in Wesser.

CHAPTER 2

Charlie's Bunion
Great Smoky Mountains National Park, North Carolina
207 miles down and 1,961 miles to go

Trimpi Shelter Register:
At first I thought, "what a cute place," sturdy shelter, yellow flowers. Then while consuming dinner the birds became active, closer. Then after having a restful sleep, I realized this isn't just "a place" - it just "is." That's what I want to be when I wake up.

Rio
GA>ME

Hmm. I wish whatever was in her oatmeal would have been in mine.

Smoo
GA>ME

When I entered the Great Smoky Mountains, I remembered my dreams of the trail from that first day of leafing through that guidebook in Atlanta. The mountains of Georgia had some beautiful peaks, but the Smokies rose from North Carolina like the spine of the earth, and I walked in the heavens for days on end. Until then the days were mostly comprised of long sweeps through valleys followed by a tough climb, all the while hoping that at the top of the climb there would be an open spot to rest and enjoy a view. Along the ridge of the Smokies, the short goal of reaching a beautiful view was absorbed into the blissful pace of the entire day. The

17

land always stretched below and away, and my boots clung to rocks that sloped down off cliffs and jagged tree lines. All day I would walk from one high peak to the next, stopping when the wind caught me just right or the sun shone off the valleys below and I would look down, more spellbound than tired, into the patches of trees, grass, and mirror lakes so far below. I would pause sometimes to lie on a rock just to feel the sunlight. I had lost the notion that sitting on the ground would make my clothes dirty or that bugs and grime and nature would invade my person and my belongings. Such a thought would be akin to fearing that a thread may fall from my clothes or that a crumb may fall from my plate. The barrier between me and the mountains was evaporating.

The first days of spring in the Smokies were a bit colder than the tail of winter in Georgia. It seemed the temperature only stretched above freezing in the middle of the day, and I would start out in the morning wearing the thick, white polar-fleece pullover my cousin had made for me. The fleece was the envy of everyone I met in those days, not much to look at, but obviously as warm as an entire flock of sheep. After I had been hiking for an hour or so, my body was hot enough to be comfortable on all but the coldest, windiest, rainiest of days, and the pullover would come off.

In the mornings, I arranged my stove and cooking gear while still in my sleeping bag. Even when I kept my water bottles in the bag against my body to keep them from freezing, I would pour the water into my aluminum pan only to watch it turn to an icy sludge before I got my stove going, and oatmeal had to be eaten quickly before it became cold and hard. With the chill, though, came an unparalleled crispness that revealed faraway mountains as if tiny particles of ice in the air were magnifying the light. During a hike, that cold air was a blessing and a curse, freezing the nose and throat one minute, cooling an overheated torso the next. It could be hard to bear without the sun, but I was blessed with more sunlight than rain along the ridge, and those days of hiking along the peaks of North Carolina made me feel like a king with the mountains for my crown.

In the Smokies, as in most national parks, camping is restricted to designated shelters and campsites, and campers are strongly advised to use the shelters strapped with chain-link fences to keep out the bears. I had heard stories about bears tearing open the fencing to free a trapped cub, but never just to get at a camper's food. Mice, on the other hand, treated the shelters like a cross between a theme park and a buffet. At dusk they could be seen bouncing towards the shelter from the woods, finding hiding places among the rocks where they would wait for the hikers to settle in before beginning their scavenging patrols. At night I would wake up as a mouse bounced across my forehead or began chewing loudly into some paper nearby. Once I looked over in the shaded moonlight of the shelter to see a mouse perched on the lips of the hiker next to me, eating scraps of food from his moustache. The food bags were hung on strings from the roof with tuna cans threaded just above the bag. The idea was that when mice climbed down the string and tried to go around the can, it would tip and they would fall. It worked most of the time. At the foot of the sleeping platform, the row of food bags would string along like hanging bean pods with cylinders of various tuna or bean can discs shielding their thin strings.

On Georgia's Blood Mountain there was a famous skunk that patrolled the shelter and would even use the sleeping hikers as runways to launch himself at the hanging food bags. The night I spent there a hiker's dog had met the skunk, so instead of dealing with the skunk's scavenging, we dealt with a miserable dog that had been sprayed in the snout. Backpacks were left with all the zippers open in the hope the mice and other scavengers would indulge any curiosity without chewing a hole in the pack wall. Anything edible would be visited, and any good nest material like toilet paper or the pages of a book were possible victims. The mice ran the night show, but as Squirrelfight would later say, "Hey, they live here. We're just visiting."

Shelters are spaced every six or eight miles in the Smokies, and since there is a fine for not camping in designated spots, each day offers the option of hiking the short day of six to eight miles to the next shelter, or the long day of twelve to sixteen. In the months ahead, most hikers routinely hiked fifteen or sixteen miles even through the high mountains, but in the beginning only a few were willing to go so fast or long. I was one of them, since I needed to average fifteen miles a day to finish the entire trail before school started again in the fall. Another was Bicycle Man, a hydro-geologist from Tennessee.

We met in Fontana Dam, the small resort town at the southern edge of Great Smoky Mountain National Park. Hikers clustered there to collect mail drops from the post office and look for town food among the sparsely populated village. Because of a small forest fire along the edge of the park where the trail climbed from the dam to the height of the ridge, we were delayed in leaving, and a sizeable group of hikers gathered by the time the trail was opened. It was the off season, so almost all the stores were closed, but I was able to get some chicken and dumplings from the lodge, served by what seemed like a maintenance worker who may have cooked it himself in the back and pocketed the money since I never heard or saw another soul and the place seemed closed.

When we got the okay to enter the park, I did my best to fill out the back-country permit that asked for times and dates that I would be in each shelter, and left a copy with the ranger station. The eight of us who had been backed up there struck out together, stringing along the steep climb up the ridge past smoldering logs and still-flaming trees, the air thin and corrosive. That night was incredibly noisy, with all eight hikers crammed in the tiny shelter. Between the snoring and the scurrying of the mice and a possible rat, it was quite a chore to go to sleep. The second day there were only five of us who had hiked to the second shelter, and after that day, Bicycle Man and I were the only ones hiking the long day. The shelters were otherwise empty.

Bicycle Man was a kind, quiet man who seemed completely unaffected by the cold. We spoke lightly and seldom, the chatter of the forest always a third party in our days' long, lightly visited conversation. He had done fieldwork in Greenland and had no sympathy to offer me when it came to temperatures just below freezing. In the evenings he would strip down behind the shelter and wash the sweat off of himself with a wet bandanna, despite the frigid air and biting wind. It gave me icy flashbacks to washing my socks in the stream. I grew up in the South and preferred ending the cold days by covering myself with polar-fleece and rain jacket and letting body heat dry up the sweat in my clothes, even if I had to wear them in my sleeping bag all night. The thought of putting on a shirt in the morning that had frozen stiff in the night like those socks did seemed far worse than sleeping in my own sweat day after day.

Bicycle Man was a very light sleeper and was willing to sleep in his tent outside the shelter with the bears rather than spend a sleepless night because of someone's snoring. He set up his tent the first night we were alone and then slept in the shelter so that if I started snoring he could quickly relocate, but it was a quiet night and after that he just left his tent packed up. In the mornings we would rise when the sun lit the camp. Bicycle Man would eat a quick, cold breakfast and pack up his gear while I set up my stove from the warmth of my sleeping bag and cooked oatmeal. Bicycle Man would start hiking fifteen or twenty minutes before me each morning, leaving me in the shelter trying to scoop out little scraps of my oatmeal before they froze to the pan. My pace is somewhat slower than most, but once I get going I'll continue for long stretches before stopping. In a few hours I would see Bicycle Man sitting on a log, eating a granola bar, and looking thoughtfully into the trees.

"Wayah the Wolf," Bicycle Man would call out when there were only a dozen yards or so left between us. His voice had a little squeak to it and cascaded down as he said the name.

"The Wolf is upon ya," I would say, stopping for a moment to talk about things we had seen that morning, or about the stretch of trail ahead, and then I would keep on walking, leaving Bicycle Man behind until I stopped for lunch at the half-way shelter and Bicycle Man caught up. We would sit on the porch and eat our bread, peanut butter, candy bars, and any other food we could spare. While we ate, we would pass the shelter register back and forth to read the comments and thoughts of hikers who had already passed through, and add our own thoughts and observations. The registers had changed from simple data books to chronicles of the hikers who were ahead. Very few were hikers that had passed me since I was going farther than the average at the time, but certain hikers up ahead regularly had interesting or funny things to say, and the more I read their entries, the more I felt I knew them even though they had never heard of me. Likewise, as I lay down my thoughts, I had no idea who was behind me reading them and might one day catch up, knowing my name and thoughts, experiences and opinions.

The day before the end of the Smokies, Bicycle Man planned to meet his girlfriend where a road crossed the trail, and leave for a few days off with her. There was a parking lot where motorists could get out and enjoy the view, use the bathrooms, or access the trail. Bicycle Man had talked about the cookies and goodies she would bring him and spent quiet moments thinking about the rest. His daily comments about getting away from the trail, even for a short break, had felt heavy in the sparse field of our conversation, and between me and the forest, he had left long before coming to the wide, overpopulated roadside vista. I said good-bye to them and walked quickly away from the uncomfortably crowded parking lot where dozens of passersby had stopped to look off of the ridge where I lived. Five hundred miles would pass underfoot before I would see Bicycle Man again, and we would hardly recognize each other.

Four miles from the road is a point called Charlie's Bunion. The path to it is beaten wide and the rocks smooth from the people who are willing to hike the miles from the road to have a glimpse. As I sloped up higher on the ridge, uneasiness fluttered about me like a small moth. The return of the isolation that had transformed me in past weeks was familiar but not quite welcome.

I hardly knew anything about Bicycle Man, but he was the only person I knew anything about. Darting past pack-less tourists over the four miles to the bunion only made me feel more alone. None of them knew any trail etiquette: to get out of the way of a hiker going up-hill so as not to kill his momentum, to always yield to anyone with a full pack. They just stood there gasping on the trail like this lightly-graded slope was some killer climb. Nearing the bunion, I filled my bottle from Icewater Spring, not bothering to filter the water that bubbled right out of the mountain's crest, and made my way out to Charlie's Bunion along the precipitous path etched into the rock to allow access to what looked like a giant's thumb sticking out of the mountain. Without stopping to put on my fleece, I laid my pack near the crease where the spike jutted out sideways from the mountain's peak and stepped out onto the ledge, the mountain dropping off vertically all around. My boots rooted solid into the cracks of the rock, and the wind whipped over and around and through me as I stretched to my full, pack-free height. I was aware of every hair on my body as the wind caressed their roots and turned the sweat that covered me and dripped from me into shells and pearls of ice. I was so awakened that I kept breathing in, and it seemed I would never breathe out. My eyes rolled back and closed as I tilted my head back for a mighty howl.

"Are you a thru-hiker?" I almost tumbled off the precipice as I swallowed the howl whole and nearly lost my balance. Craning slowly around I saw three adolescent girls with two parents clambering up behind them. They looked strange with their clean clothes and smooth, soft hair, like dolls or vacation photographs. I nodded suspiciously, unsure what they planned to do to me. I felt trapped on the narrow cliff.

"That's so cool!" The girls began at once chattering excitedly amongst themselves and to me, but I couldn't follow a word of it. I couldn't believe they were speaking my native language. Their sentences were fast and peppered with nonsense, spilling out like coins from a slot machine. I realized that I was less like a person in a conversation than an animal viewed on safari, and that the glass was foggy and thick.

"Can I take your picture? A thru-hiker." I looked at the father with weary confusion. Everyone I knew was a thru-hiker. I was just the one who had gotten himself caught. Behind the parents a little girl climbed unsteadily onto the rocks.

"Honey," said the father, bending over the girl to speak softly, "this man is hiking 2,000 miles. How far have you gone so far?" He looked up at me grinning. I looked down into the child's eyes, and they seemed very real, like the wind and the mountains. She was smiling a little and seeing me and the rocks and the sky without any filter or assumption.

"A couple hundred," I said, eyes still locked with the child. She must be one of us, I thought. She's really here, not back with the car or the house or the TV or what someone said a few minutes ago. I could feel her speak before the word came.

"Why?" she said frankly. For the father I might have tried to think of something clever. He would have laughed, or there would have been *ooh*'s and *hmm*'s, and the family would have left with their experience complete and compartmentalized. But for the girl, I answered truthfully:

"I don't know."

CHAPTER 3

Hot Springs, North Carolina
270 miles down and 1,898 miles to go

Trimpi Shelter Register:
Sulu and I went into town where we purchased a glider and are hoping to fly from I-81 to Katahdin. Strawberry cheesecake shake in Troutdale greatest thing since ziploc bags. On to camp with fellow bozos. Flower Power! Would be nice to see you, girl. Wrongway, come back to Jamaica, man. Cheerio All.

Father Time
GA>ME

Pine Swamp Brook Lean-to Register:
Attention Thru Hikers!! The grocery store in town is apparently closed for good. I did manage to get some fruit (yes!) at the restaurant/bakery. I also got a quart of milk, a little pizza thing with garlic and parmesan, and a croissant which I ate on this nice bench facing the river and covered bridge. I also ate some chili & sausage.

Apparatus
GA>ME

On April fourth I woke not to the sun beaming through the trees onto the nylon wall of my tent, but to rain falling on my face through the dark. The day before, I had come upon Fly and Aces lying on top of Max Patch, an out-of-place, treeless hill in North Carolina. They were relaxing with their lunch and assorted daydreams, and I had felt compelled to join them. They were a young, trail-worn couple that carried their excitement around like concealed squirt guns. The day had sped by for us, talking, hiking and laughing. A long and difficult climb had disappeared over a discussion of *Star Wars*, and at the end of that unseasonably warm day we all ended up on top of Bluff Mountain, sleeping out on our tarps instead of in tents so we could watch the stars. Before that night it had never occurred to me to just lay my sleeping bag on top of my tarp and sleep in the wind, but Fly spoke of it as something one always did on a night such as that one, which was only chilly instead of freezing, and so I followed along without question. We were ten miles from Hot Springs, North Carolina and I was still on schedule, earning me a day of rest in town, the first in the three weeks since I began.

The weather moves quickly across the mountaintops on windy nights. When I opened my eyes after the first few drops hit me, I just lay there, looking at the blackness that had eaten the stars while I slept. I lay patiently, hopefully, not wanting to admit that it might actually be raining on me. Here and there around me came the tapping sounds of a shifting leaf, a drop of water impacting a plastic tarp; the hits almost imperceptibly picking up momentum. The rain was definitely coming. I closed my eyes and wondered if waking up in a wet sleeping bag that morning would be any worse than having to get up now and make my camp rain-proof at whatever exhausted, blackened hour this was. A large drop in my eye woke me from my dilemma.

"Aces."

"Unh?" came a strained groan from a few yards off.

"Aces, it's raining."

"Unh? Oh, mmm." I could almost hear the stages of rain denial playing out in Aces' head before he got a good one in the eye, too. "Oh, man. Fly, wake up, it's raining. Where's that headlamp? Good God, what time is it?" I saw the crisp snap of indigo through the night.

"It's four."

I got up quickly and stuffed my sleeping bag in its sack, stowing it under the fluttering rain cover of the backpack. It was cold in the dark outside the sleeping bag, and the rain was even colder. The quick movements were sharp and painful to my sore limbs and aching joints. I dug around in my pack and rooted out my raincoat and pants, quickly sliding them on over my clothes. I strapped on my headlamp and pulled the hood of the raincoat over it, angling the beam downwards to keep from blinding my friends. A few bits and pieces thrown together quickly, the ground cloth, the water bottle, and everything was packed and covered. The flurry of activity had tethered to an end, and the three of us stood staring at each other in the night. The rain glittered like cave dust in the crisscrossed paths of the three headlamps. Waterproof, awake, and packed up, we stood quietly staring into the center of the circle. Aces turned his lamp to the three packs leaning against the trees. He was a tall, thin man, with a prickly face that I knew had to be smiling by now, though it was hard to see behind the headlamp. Fly was short and wiry, and her hands dug comfortably into her hips as she acknowledged our predicament. The night had us in check. All we could do was start hiking. So just after four a.m. on the fourth day of the fourth month, three tired, wet hikers set off without breakfast to trudge through the dark rain toward town.

We walked by the light of the headlamps, watching the rain turn over the dust on the darkening ground. I went ahead and ate the last of my food when we took a break to take off layers as the sky began to lighten and the rain slacked off to almost nothing. I had been holding back my hunger for a while now, and eating the last, dusty bits of trail mix and the piece of fruit leather that I had continued to put off in each attempt to ration my remaining food, I could feel a tightening ache in my stomach, relieved only by the knowledge that up ahead was a new food drop, a restaurant, and a grocery store.

Nearing the end of the Smoky Mountains two days before, I realized that I had been eating much more of my food than in the previous mail drops and that I had about fifty miles left to Hot Springs and only a day of food left. Covering the miles as fast as I could, I landed at a shelter on the way out of the Smokies as dark set in to find the two wooden palettes completely packed with sleeping pads and bags. There was a large group of thru-hikers I had never met and three weekenders that were in the process of unloading their heavy packs. As I was contemplating the ordeal of setting up my tent in the dark here or farther down the trail after what had already been an eighteen-mile day without enough food, I overheard one of the weekenders saying, "How far are we hiking tomorrow?"

"Six miles."

"That's not too bad. We did almost that just now, right?"

"No, man. That was a mile and a half." The first weekender almost collapsed. Their packs were enormous expedition packs that were filled to capacity. They were wearing jeans and cotton shirts that would chafe and take forever to dry from their considerable sweat. As they began unpacking their gear two more hikers came from the north without packs causing great joy among the assembled thru-hikers. They began distributing foil-wrapped cheeseburgers to their crew. I couldn't take it. I grabbed one of the two that had come up the mountain.

"Where did you get those?"

"There's a little place a couple miles down the trail and then down the road east called Mountain Mamma's. They've got some killer burgers and it turns out they've got cots, but our group and gear were all back here." That was it. I would add a few more miles to this already long day to get a cheeseburger and a cot. I could hear a thru-hiker with a large mop of ratty hair saying to one of the weekenders, "That's a mighty big food bag you got there. Whatcha packin'?"

"We've got the basics. Nothing fancy." The weekender began laying out large bags of food: a three-pound bag of Peanut M&Ms, a five-pound tub of peanut butter, huge tins of tuna fish. "It's okay if some is left over. We're roommates, and we'll just pop it back on the shelves when we get home."

"No, man. You're not going to make it home. You're going to die out here if you don't unload some of that food. Here, let me sort out exactly what you need." Hikers moved in like swarming rats to help the struggling weekenders by siphoning off their "dangerous" excess weight. I managed to get an extra dinner and more M&Ms for my trail mix, but I could feel the thickening ache of night moving into my bones and I knew that if I was going to do more hiking, I needed to get to it.

Down the dark trail I trudged, my feet heavy and tired, my knees throbbing from the last six miles of constant downhill on the way off of the Smoky Mountain Ridge. I finally reached the road, bright grey in the starlight, and pulled myself along a little further until I could see the horizontal lines of a man-made structure and the warm glow of light through windows. The place seemed closed, and sure enough the door was locked, but I could see a few people inside, and I knocked and waited, hoping for grace from the Mountain Mamma. When they saw it was a hiker, the door opened and they acted as if it was no inconvenience at all. Of course we'll make you a burger, and sure you can stay here. I had only come across a few establishments that were near the trail, but I was finding with each one that they had special warmth for hikers, a generosity and kindness that were otherwise reserved from the average outsider. Though the burger involved a microwave and the cot was little more comfortable than my tent, my belly was full of hot food that I hadn't carried and I was resting under the roof of hospitality. I slept well and hard.

I bought a breakfast at Mountain Mamma's, and the extra trail mix had helped stretch my food through the next day. I ate the weekenders' dinner that night with Fly and Aces and went to bed with a grumbling stomach, watching the stars. I had eaten the smallest crumbs, the dust from each bag, and scraped each jar clean, and all that was left was a few miles' march to relief.

As I rounded the last bluff with Fly and Aces on that unseasonably warm and wet morning, I finally saw the manmade lines of Hot Springs nestled among the creases in the mountains below us. One main street wound through the village, but waiting in the tiny buildings below were all the comforts of society and a much-needed day of rest. Down the slope and on the street through town we quickly tucked ourselves into the town's small diner to feast on burgers, fries, milkshakes, and tater tots until the pain of hunger was finally replaced by the heavy expanse of gluttony. Returning to the street, Fly and Aces veered off to a bed-and-breakfast mentioned in the *Thru-hiker's Handbook*. I went on to the post office to pick up my supplies saying I'd meet them at the inn later. It wasn't quite noon, and the sun had driven high over the hills as the day turned warm, baking the street and drying the rain into trails of lingering steam. The nostalgic smell of wet asphalt with a hint of exhaust drifted over the road as I made my way to the post office to pick up the package my mother had sent with mail and supplies for the next stretch.

The post office was clean and cold with lots of hard edges and sterile surfaces. I pulled off my pack and leaned it against the wall with some reluctance since it seemed so out of place. It was pleasantly light and hollow since it had no food weight, and the sound of the frame tapping on the hard floor seemed very loud in this silent place. The woods can be called quiet and peaceful, but between the wind, the trees, and the animals, it's rarely silent. The strange, steady stillness of the stone reception area felt foreign. The postmaster answered the shiny bell from the recesses of a room filled with shelves and letters and packages. Suddenly in close quarters with a town person, I was bombarded by smells of soap, shampoo, and aftershave. The smells were not entirely unpleasant, but they were strikingly unnatural and a little overwhelming. The postmaster seemed to be having a similar olfactory experience being in close quarters with a thru-hiker, but was more practiced in his reaction. He was kind and steady, and he brought a brown cardboard box to the counter that was addressed to the post office. It had "Please hold for Through-Hiker" written all over it.

"I'll just need to see your ID," said the postmaster. I reached into a pouch where all of my important cards were tied together with a rubber band making them lighter and smaller than a wallet. I shuffled through the credit card, insurance card, and phone card, finally reaching the driver's license. I looked at the face and the name on the license for a moment after he returned it. I had a full head of thick hair in the picture and looked so clean. So unlike Wayah the Wolf. With three weeks of growth now, my short, oily hairs were pressed flat under my cap and what little facial hair I had was beginning to curl. My skin was already beginning to harden from the sun and oil and salt. I signed in briefly at the post office's hiker register, which was more cursory than a shelter register since it was more for location purposes. Supposedly if someone were trying to find a hiker, the rangers could call post offices to find the first place they hadn't signed in and then hike backwards from there, talking to hikers and checking registers to close in on the correct location.

I made my way back out into the air and hauled both pack and cardboard box across the road to the bed-and-breakfast to get a room, unpack, and prepare for a day off. The inn had been the refuge of many hikers through the years. The cost was very low for hikers, and the place was made to feel real and substantial. It was like being welcomed into someone's home instead of paying for lodging. I climbed up the creaky wooden stairs to a room I would share with another thru-hiker named Kaptain Krummholz, who wasn't in the room at the time. I proceeded to uncurl the tightness and ache from my body and cut open the box that had come in the mail. Inside were Ziploc bags full of food, letters, and some replacement clothing. It had probably been packed very neatly, but the voyage had tossed it into a pleasantly chaotic collage of comfort. I rummaged through the food first. It didn't look like enough. When I had started the trail three weeks earlier, the food space in my pack held enough for nine or ten days, but with my new level of consumption, it would be much less. I couldn't imagine the food in front of me being adequate. My next stop in Elk Park was eight days away, and my stomach groaned as I looked at the box. Four packs of oatmeal, four packs of toaster pastries, eight packs of hot chocolate, twenty-six candy bars, a jar of peanut butter, a pound of summer sausage, a block of cheese, a large bag of gorp (which stands for "Good Ol' Raisins and Peanuts," but more commonly takes the form of nuts, granola, chocolate, raisins, and anything else one decides to mix in), six Lipton noodle dinners, and two bags of rice and spices. There was no way it would be enough. Before I had started hiking it had looked like so much food, but now it looked to last five or six days at best. Ooo! There was a bag full of gummy critters near the bottom. I picked them out and began to chew on them while I finished sorting through the box. The gummies were too heavy to carry considering what poor fuel they were, but they would do nicely as a treat to keep me alive until dinner.

Beginning to feel very comfortable in the room, I leaned back in a chair to read my mail with the sun streaming through the old window. There was a desk with books and pictures on it, and because I felt that this was my room, they felt like my things. There was a comfort that came from feeling like the master of my environment, and I realized again how isolated I had been. The pain in my body was falling gently away. My eyes caught a long, thin map of the Eastern seaboard on the wall. It had "Appalachian Trail" written across the

33

top and a thick red line zigzagging its way down the middle. I dropped the letters back in the box, glanced at the lower half of the map and found myself looking at Virginia. Farther down was North Carolina, and at the bottom of North Carolina was Hot Springs.

"You're kidding me," I said aloud, thinking of the 270 miles I had hiked and looking at the tiny tail of trail behind me and the great dragon before me.

The ache of my feet echoed about the room. Pulling my thoughts back together I walked past the back of the room through a doorway to where one of the floor's bathrooms was. Not only was this the cleanest place to poop I had seen in weeks, but it had a luxuriously deep bathtub with bath salts and soaps. I almost forgot to close the door before stripping down and filling up the tub to begin soaking away some of the weariness. I watched the rim of dirt that started above my socks begin to fade away, leaving only my deepening hiker tan line. My pale and wrinkly toes swelled and tingled painfully at the foreign rush of blood. By the time I was finished I needed to drain the tub and then rinse it out again to remove all the dirt. In the bottom of the clothing pouch of my backpack was an untouched Ziplock bag containing a pair of clean cotton boxers and a clean cotton T-shirt. They didn't clench tight, stick, or catch, they only hung softly on my body like a good listener, and I sat for a while in the window just being clean and quiet. When I finally decided to venture downstairs I found that walking barefoot was very difficult. It felt like the bones in my feet were broken or bruised, and I was losing the feeling in the tips of my toes, but it was so nice to walk on the cold, clean wood without my suffocating boots that I decided to bear the discomfort. I thought that resting this afternoon and tomorrow might give my feet enough time to heal, but actually it would be seven more months before I would be able to walk barefoot without limping or to feel any of my toes.

Tenderly down the ornate staircase and gently around the corner, I sought out a shape I thought I had seen upon entering the inn. Sure enough, there was a guitar propped up by a large comfortable couch. In fact the room was a music room, with a variety of instruments and many other chairs, but the guitar was what I sought. Sitting and playing was euphoric. The old, cluttered living room with its high ceiling and huge windows was shady and cool, and the lacy curtains caught reflections of the sleepy country light through the open shutter. I could smell the spring air outside and the rich, warm smell of baking bread coming from the kitchen in the back. The other instruments, leaning in corners and tucked behind old furniture, listened quietly while I strummed and sang, my eyes closed and smiling.

"Hey man, is that 'Blackbird' I hear? Good tuuune," came a weary voice. I had learned the Beatles song just before starting the trail and was picking it out slowly. I looked up and saw a vaguely familiar figure. He was dressed in white cotton slacks and a sweater, but his limp, sweat-stained hat and obviously tired body gave him away as a thru-hiker. "What's up? I'm Jones." He drew out the "o" to perch on his lips with what sounded to me like a slight surfer accent. It was still a little awkward, introducing ourselves to people by our trail names.

"I'm Wayah." I rested my arms on top of the guitar remembering Jones now as one of the hikers I had passed at the full shelter before Mountain Mamma's. "I passed you guys three days ago in Davenport Gap. It was dark and the shelter was full, so I moved on to Mountain Mamma's. You must've passed me the next morning before I got up."

"Bummer, man. Yeah, me and Squirrel and Flux shot outta there pre-dawn so we could get close enough yesterday to get in here for breakfast this morning. Keep jammin', dude." Jones sat down in the heavy chair next to the couch where I was sitting. "Ohh, it feels good to be off these feet." I went back to playing, and now and then Jones would chime in.

It was approaching suppertime and the smell of rich foods poured from the kitchen, making our stomachs roll. It was hard to believe that so soon after being stuffed to satisfaction we could feel the ache of intense hunger again, but our bodies had begun processing fuel at a rate to match our sustained activity. With the nearing of dinner we were joined by others gathering for the approaching meal. Some were coming from chores taken to offset the already small cost of staying at the inn, and others from long baths or naps. Fly and Aces came in with a hiker named Squirrelfight, and I could see that they knew each other well. Squirrelfight was perhaps the scruffiest person I had seen yet. He had a curly, light brown beard and long, thick, frayed braids of hair that stuck out like a mop. Flux, Cain, and Snow Leopard also came in, and soon everyone had picked up an instrument or made a drum out of some furniture or gear. Fly and Aces introduced me to the rest of the group, most of whom had been at the Davenport Gap shelter when I passed. I balked less and less at hearing the hikers say "Wayah" to me and to each other as the afternoon wore into evening, and felt the Wolf growing in power as he became whole.

We all played and laughed and sang a motley, improvised tune. Fly found a hat rack in an adjoining room covered with strange hats and masks and brought one out for each of us. We fell together easily, talking, joking, and playing. We had everything in common with each other and nothing in common with anyone else. The world before the trail was becoming a series of irrelevant details, but the shelters we had passed, the people we had met, the mountains and weather we had shared—those were the details that made up the life we knew. I couldn't believe how happy I was. I had been holding a quiet loneliness inside that had been growing in the past weeks. It melted away as darkness fell and dampened, antiquated lamps flooded the parlor. In its wake I waded in a warm sea of friendship, unified towards the single purposes of joy and dinner.

The meal was a work of art, sculpted with thru-hikers in mind. Bottomless dishes were full of the fresh vegetables we had been missing, and the tastes and textures were of a royal, authentic sort, extraordinary even off the trail. I sat at the end of the table by Jones and Squirrelfight, prodding Jones with stories and jokes, enjoying his laughter. Squirrel was eating fiercely and smiling, but not hearing all of the joking over the grinding of his jowls. We met other hikers that night, including the mysterious Kaptain Krummholz, though despite the fact we shared a bed that night, some time would pass before I would hike with him and come to know him well. Long after our bellies were full we continued piling the delicacies onto our plates and measuring them into our mouths as space presented itself. Our stomachs stuffed with warm, good food, we finally pulled ourselves from the table and dragged off into lit rooms to talk and laugh into the night. We shared stories of fright, luck, embarrassment, and mischief. Jones was so full, he was having trouble laughing and couldn't even drink the beer he had bought for after dinner. Only a couple had seen any bears yet, and they were envied. A few told stories of friends who had recently called it quits. These stories were solemn, because those that left were not so different from those gathered here, and their struggles were familiar.

These hikers were not like the ones I had met during those first days on the trail. They each had a month and 270 miles of trail behind them now, and their lives were only subtle variants of mine. They had seen the same trails, felt the same rain, knew the woods as their homes, and were learning, as I was, how simple the joys of life really are. I wanted to keep laughing, to keep sharing stories, to keep feeling Wayah the Wolf. As I listened to Squirrelfight telling the story of Jones trying to hitchhike into town cradling a leaking bottle of syrup, and his conversation with the owners of the BMW that eventually pulled over, Jones slapped his knee, his face paralyzed with laughter. I decided that I had had enough of being alone for a while; these hikers were the best company I could imagine. Realizing that they planned to continue on the next day while I was looking forward to my blissful day of rest, I pleaded with them to stay another day with me so we could continue on together. Jones, Jokers, and Squirrelfight agreed.

CHAPTER 4

Apple House Shelter, Tennessee
381 miles down and 1,787 miles to go

Doc's Knob Shelter Register:
These last few days of walking in the gloom and rain have fueled a lot of heavy thought. I won't try to record it all here, but in hearing of friends and acquaintances ahead and behind who have had to leave the trail for one reason or another, I have been thinking of what it must mean to end such a journey prematurely. I think it all depends on why a person is out here to begin with. When I started my hike, my view of the trail was that it was something to be finished. If I had quit then, it would have been like a failure. Since then I have learned that the trail is an experience. To have been a part of it is all that matters. Each day we move closer to the end, but I reached my goal that day in the Nantahalas when I realized what I was a part of here. I intend to finish the trail, but to leave would be no tragedy. Every day can be as rich as a day on the trail, no matter who you are. This is the most important thing I have learned, as Thoreau put it, "to live deliberately."

May you all learn from the trail, whatever the lesson, and grow from being a part of it, even if not for 2000 miles.

Wayah the Wolf
GA>ME

Jones tossed his poking stick in the fire as he laughed, trying not to howl as there were friends asleep in the shelter and tents nearby. He sat on a log next to Squirrelfight and struggled for breath, his hand clutching his stomach. Squirrel couldn't stop either; his hair and beard framed a laugh that was as much a grimace as a smile, with tears starting to squeeze from his tightly shut eyes. I sat across from them on the ground, stomach vibrating, an endless, silent laugh stuck to my face. Jokers Wild had wandered off into the dark to relieve himself and to fish out one of the cheap beers they had carried in from town and weighed down in the stream to cool. There were only a few left now that it was late, and the other hikers in the shelter had already had their fill and retired. The empty cans were in a pile to be hoisted out of reach with the rest of the food and trash. He had been gone a while now, and we had begun to speculate about what he might be up to. His many additional years of hiking experience had led to a comfort in the woods that included a long list of pranks and shortcuts that often caught the rest of us off guard. Many of them seemed so practiced and elegant that they must surely be some form of distilled perfection, like secreting rocks or trash in our packs during a short break only to retrieve them after an especially hard climb saying, "Thanks for carrying that for me!" Others were a little off-putting, like hitchhiking ahead after falling behind, missing whole sections of the trail, a practice known as "Yellow-Blazing."

The larger group of hikers that traveled through the Smokies and entered Hot Springs with Squirrelfight, Jones, and Jokers were all ahead of us now after we stayed the extra day in Hot Springs. It didn't help that the first day out of town we'd come to a beautiful waterfall only three miles into our day and decided to make it our camp since it seemed a crime to just walk by such a beautiful place. The four of us had been hiking and camping together for the ten days since. Ten days wasn't much before the trail, but in the woods, seeing each other most of the day every day, a week seemed like months. We would talk and hike, sit and watch, listen and sing. We were able to learn a lot about each other in those few days with so much exposure and so few barriers. Jones was very comfortable talking about how horny he was, Squirrelfight would amuse himself by repeating a movie quote over and over with different inflections, and Jokers had a terrible singing voice but loved to sing. I was also coming to know some of what was underneath my fellow hikers. Jones had lost his father when he was young and there was a hollowness in him that was angrily covered up, Squirrelfight had loved hard and lost hard, and could not let go, and Jokers was not headed where he wanted in his life but didn't know how to get there. When we gathered to indulge the hike like this, though, all the empty places were filled. It had been suggested by a few other hikers that the four of us come up with a group name. We hadn't met many continuous groups. There were a lot of pairs or couples, but in the days ahead, we would rarely find groups that had hiked together as long as we did. I was the youngest member of the group at twenty-one. Jones and Squirrelfight were twenty-three and just out of college, while Jokers Wild was much older, already in his thirties. Six-foot-two and stocky, I was the largest by a good bit. Jones was smaller and very impressed by his new definition. When he started the trail, he had been carrying quite a bit more body fat, but now he had slimmed down and was showing some sturdy muscle. He always wore his white cap, curled down at the brim like they did in his fraternity. Squirrelfight was just a little shorter than me and very lean, on his head the signature mop of tangled braids becoming dreadlocks and his face a play between laughter and one of the practiced entertainments from his years of studying theater in college. We had all been laughing for quite a while, our bellies filled with dinner, and now the momentum of the silliness needed only an occasional shove, which I was happy to give.

"Stop! Please stop!" Jones managed to choke out between gasps, "You're killing me. I'm gonna die!" Out of the darkness came Jokers' wiry, thickly-bearded figure. After finding the beer, he had gone to secretly stash the crushed, empty cans from the evening's celebration under Jones' tent, directly beneath the sleeping bag, and was ready to get back to the warmth of the fire and join in the laughter again.

Even though we were camping every day, a campfire was an uncommon event. Most nights we would come in just before dark, and the hissing of four little white gas stoves would replace some of the chatter as we tried to get supper cooked before losing the daylight. After a day's hike we were usually too tired to make a fire or to stay awake long enough for it to die down properly to reduce the risk of forest fire. That night before Easter, though, we had a good fire. We had stopped in Elk Park, Tennessee, that morning to have a big breakfast at a local restaurant and pick up supplies and mail from the post office. After spending an hour or so sorting food and then shopping at the town store for the bread and other supplies that hadn't come in the mail drops (and having a bit of ice cream), we headed for the phone and the all-you-can-eat diner down the road. By the time we were finished there, bellies well rounded and heads swimming with contentment, it was past noon. The section of trail ahead was unique because the locals had a particular dislike of the hikers and were known to be hostile and sometimes violent. The postmaster had urged us to move through the area quickly, not to stop for at least thirteen miles, and not to drink any water over that stretch. The locals had been known to pour gas or oil in the streams to poison them. It was hard to believe after all the hospitality we had seen that a town would collectively decide to hate hikers that way. A few years ago there had even been an assault when locals came to burn down a shelter near their town and found a hiker there. Nothing particularly bad had happened since then, but the hostility was still tangible and the proximity was dangerously uncomfortable. We would have to carry a lot of water to cover all those miles in the heat and humidity that had built up rather suddenly in the past few days since the Smokies. Normally we would start the day with a full load of water, weighing about eight pounds, and refill during the day and in the evening. Not refilling in the middle of the day, especially a hot one, meant carrying extra bottles. Since we only carried a few quart bottles, we had purchased containers of Gatorade in the town store to fill with additional water. The cheap plastic wouldn't hold up long, but it would do as temporary water storage. As we came out of the store, there was some doubt as to whether or not we could make it with what remained of the day. It was hot, we were stuffed, and thirteen was a lot to do after lunch anyway, more so with full packs and extra water. It wasn't very hard to convince each other to go back down the trail to the shelter and take the afternoon off. That also gave us more time to relax in town.

We decided to make phone calls and buy some food for the afternoon and some cheap beer for the night. Then we headed back to the Apple House Shelter where we had stayed the night before. On the way back down the road to the trailhead, a car pulled over behind us. Considering the reputation of the area, we were a bit nervous, but in fact it was a thru-hiker from years past, named Jump Start because he had parachuted down to the beginning of the trail to start his hike. He gave us some apples, played his harmonica for us, and told us to say hi to Rusty for him before disappearing down the road again. It would be a long time before we reached Rusty's famous hostel, but we were already beginning to hear stories about the place and see clues in shelters about how to find it. The stories seemed conflicted— some about rest, some about mischief, but they were mysterious and far away still.

Back at the shelter, a few newcomers had arrived. Two British gentlemen known as Greylag and Optimist (or collectively as "the Brits") had moved into the shelter and annexed a corner of it. They were both over sixty. Every morning they soft-boiled two eggs and placed them in wooden egg holders they carried so as to eat the eggs properly. There was also a photographer going by the name of Tall Grass Prairie (or TGP). He and his partner, a writer named Curly, were hiking a section of the trail as part of a confederacy of reporters publishing a progression of stories while relay-hiking the entire trail that year. These two were covering the second leg, and Curly had fallen in love with one of the few women on the trail, Harper's Fairy, leaving the photographer behind since his feet were bothering him. TGP was a little frustrated at being left alone, and the other hikers were a little frustrated that Curly was attempting to lay claim to one of the trail's beautiful women. The stranded photographer was welcomed into the thru-hiker's camp, and he busily went about his job of documenting our activities. When Squirrel started cleaning his boots, TGP was taking pictures. When Jones wrote in his journal, TGP was taking pictures. I watched my back as I headed into the woods to use the privy.

The day wore on at a relaxed pace. It was nice to take time for leisure, but the expanse of miles ahead would always beckon when a stop wasn't absolutely necessary. We set up our tents a safe distance from the shelter since they would be a little warmer and we would be out of the mouse zone. It was not unusual for us to set up tents and cook food a hundred feet from the shelter and then watch mice run past our food on their way to their nightly shelter feast. We still camped near shelters instead of in the woods because they were built near good water sources and were the loci of our culture. I had been carrying a small roll of duct tape with me since the start, and now I used it for the first time, wrapping it into a ball. Jones dropped his sitting mat down as home plate, and we had a sporting game of duct-tape-ball using a stick for a bat. The evening found us making our fire and passing around beers. Tall Grass Prairie even put down the camera for a while to drink with us. As Optimist finished his beer and left the circle to find his sleeping bag, he mentioned that as a minister of the

Dominican order, he would be giving Easter Mass at sunup if anyone would like to be in attendance. The thought of a mass in the woods was an unusual surprise and we all promised not to miss it.

"So where do your people come from, Wayah?" Jokers asked quickly during a lull in the laughter.

"Well, my family name is German or Austrian, but my most recently migrated relatives are Norwegian." The group all nodded, looking at my large, tall frame. "My people are Vikings. I was pretty much bred to vike."

"Born to vike," Squirrelfight laughed. "I like it. That should be our name, the Vikings." We laughed into the night about the name, thinking of ways to loot and pillage along the trail, mostly a process of renaming our normal activities. Raiding villages instead of re-supplying and having a nice meal. Pillaging the world for everything that it had to offer. We felt far more like Viking raiders in the woods than we did like vacationers. Something primal about the idea seemed to fit. My sense of myself as Wayah fit much better among the Vikings than among college kids on a long hike. In the past days I had begun losing track of my old self. Wayah could do things Tanner couldn't, say things Tanner wouldn't. Wayah knew his people and was known by them more than Tanner ever had been. I liked the feel of the Wolf and now found it jolting when TGP asked for my "real" name to put on the photos in their paper and book.

The conversation slowly died down with the fire. Hikers drifted away until only Jones and Squirrelfight sat whispering. They waited into the night to watch the full moon rise that night before Easter and deposited plastic eggs full of candy into the boots and tent flaps of all the hikers. They had originally planned to hike under the full moon all night, planting the eggs in the gear of hikers they passed in the night. Unfortunately, our location that day made the task a bit unwieldy as there would be no hikers for fourteen miles, so instead they dropped the candy in the cavities and corners of their own campsite. Returning to their tents to finally rest, the sound of crushing and twisting aluminum followed by quiet cursing and laughter could be heard from Jones' tent, along with a snicker from Jokers Wild as he lay in the shelter.

Before sunrise, the camp began to stir. There was some excitement about the candy, but the focus was on Optimist, who was preparing for his service. He asked Jones to start a fire in the fire-pit, in front of which he sat with the rest of the hikers in a circle. From the fire, he lit a well-preserved candle and began the service. The campfire symbolized God, the candle flame his son. Optimist performed the Easter ceremony just as he might have in a cathedral. He had even brought blessed wine for the communion in a small vial that he had carried for the last 380 miles. He preached for a while about the significance of all the symbols and of Easter itself to the five hikers sitting around the fire. The trees bent patiently over us, the fire spun comfortably in the stone ring, and the trail waited quietly behind us. There were no two people of the same faith around that ring, but among the rocks and the trees was a peace and holiness not easily found indoors. As the service came to a close, the sun was slowly peaking over the hill beside the shelter, and the gathering was charged with a cleansing light. Thanking Optimist and filling our water bottles and the extra Gatorade bottles for the long, non-stop day ahead, we Vikings pulled on our packs, loaded down with a full food re-supply and extra water weight, and leaned down the trail hoping for a non-confrontational holiday.

As it turned out, the locals certainly weren't accepting, but they let us pass mostly without event. A man on a motorcycle with his daughter sitting daintily in his lap in her Easter dress did give us the finger as he rode by, but passing the wreckage of the burned shelter later that day and seeing the rusted oil drums in the streams, we knew that we had certainly missed the worst of what happened there. No dogs were set on us; no razor blades were strung across the trail. The worst

Viking adversaries that day were water weight and wet spring heat, which was enough. We wound up and away from the contested stretch of trail until the afternoon, when we had passed the thirteen miles and could fill our bottles again and breathe easy in the hot Easter air.

CHAPTER 5

National Rangers Association Headquarters, Virginia
514 miles down and 1,654 miles to go

Pine Swamp Branch Shelter Register:
I hereby rename this shelter "Pine Swamp Branch Davidian Shelter." I've converted the privy to a high security stockade and am locking myself in with a cache of weapons, ammunition, and rations in wait of the Apocalypse. Please do not disturb (unless you want to be saved).

Kaptain Krummholz
GA>ME

Going up and down Mt. Rogers we saw our first snow of the trail. While we climbed the mountain, mist came down thick and cold, turning to ice and then snow as the wind gathered pleasant flakes into a blinding blizzard. Barely able to find the shelter near the top, we joined a very desperate looking group of hikers that had dashed forward or turned around and hurried back to reach the shelter and get out of the blizzard. It was the only spot on the mountain that offered any real relief from the storm. The other hikers had already draped a large tarp across the open front of the shelter and tied it off tight to keep heat in and wind out as much as possible. Even so, we spent a very cold night huddled against each other, listening to our boots freeze solid while the winds howled outside and hikers moaned inside.

The next day the world was a quiet sheet of snow punctuated by lines of snow-covered trees, and down the mountainside clouds swam through the valleys. Rocks and mile signs showed the marks of the wind as if they had sprouted icy fur and the wind had molded it into a swept tableau.

We had a unique new problem.

A hiker named Scoobie had latched onto us and would not let go. We Vikings normally were happy to welcome anyone to join our camp, but Scoobie managed to push buttons we didn't know we had. He claimed to be a super-athlete in the process of yo-yoing the trail, meaning he was going to hike north and then come back south, finishing the trail twice in one year. He talked a lot about hiking twenty-five-mile days on average, but since he had joined us in Damascus, we had hiked a ten-mile day and then a five-mile day, hoping he would go on without us, but Scoobie said jovially, "I think I'll just keep slacking with you lazy bums." Then there was the insecurity. Scoobie had to one-up anything that was done or said. When Jones referred to me as a human dispose-all, handing me unwanted remains from his gorp, Scoobie took that to mean that I had a reputation for being able to eat a lot instead of for having an indiscriminate palate. He then spent the next day in a one-sided competition with me to prove he could eat more.

Even his massive insecurities may have been laughably bearable, but he was also intentionally offensive. The night before the snowstorm we shared a shelter with an older couple who were section-hiking. It would have been perfectly pleasant without Scoobie there, but he managed to drop offense after offense, until all we Vikings could do was apologize. So huddled in the icy, blizzard-tossed shelter we had come up with a plan. When the morning came and the mountain was a beautiful icy landscape, Squirrelfight said to Scoobie, "We're talking about doing a twenty-five miler today."

"It's about time," replied Scoobie with glee. "I just need to get my things ready."

"We're already packed up, so we'll get moving and you can catch up to us, okay?"

"That shouldn't be too hard," replied Scoobie with a toss of his hair. We set out right away, but stopped about a mile down the trail, bundled in our fleece and other warm gear to have a snack. When Scoobie caught up, he wasn't wearing a shirt, much like the day before during the blizzard, professing that the cold couldn't touch him. He stood there for a minute, his skin turning pink and quivering.

"Let's get going, you slackers!" he chattered out.

"In a minute, Scoob," said Jones, slowly chewing a frozen candy bar like a cow chewing its cud.

"I'm going to go on ahead. You can take my picture on those rocks up ahead. You probably won't be able to catch me until I stop to make camp, though."

"I doubt that, Scoobie," said Squirrelfight. "We'll see you in a few."

Scoobie shot down the trail with the fresh energy of Squirrel's challenge, and we sat like watching raiders as he wound up the peak. The last time we saw Scoobie, he struck a gallant pose for us against the backdrop of the Grayson Highlands, but we didn't take a picture. We played all day, only hiking a few miles over the Highlands where wild ponies ran through the melting, speckled snow. When we got to the next shelter at the bottom of the mountain, we stopped and made an early, chilly camp.

We were down to three since Jokers Wild had stayed in Damascus a few days earlier to wait for mail and promised to catch up soon. I had sent my gloves back home in the mail from Damascus. I had walked through the bitter cold of the Smokies without ever wearing them and things had been getting much warmer up till then. Later that day, I had needed to go to the outfitter for a sturdier pack since mine was not only beginning to fall apart, but was gouging my sides with improbably placed metal screws. The outfitter had offered me a walking stick from a barrel, and I had picked one out that fit my hand and had some nice places on it for carving and engraving. Now in the cold again I realized that the reason I hadn't needed the gloves was that my hands had been in my pockets. Having been out all day holding onto the stick in the cold, I was prepared to sit on my hands for a week if that was how long it took to get the feeling back. I had switched hands whenever one went numb, but often the pocketed hand hadn't had time to warm up when its turn came around. Squirrelfight, dubbed Viking Hero for his acts of inspirational valor, took pictures madly all day and then sat in the shelter writing in his journal, trying to remember everything we had done and seen that day. Jones, the Viking Destroyer, was starting a campfire, the ceremonial duty from which he got his name.

Down from the high altitude of the night before, the temperatures were steadily warming, and though the nights might grow cold even on a warm day, it would be a long while before we would be as cold again as we were in the Grayson Highlands. I poured some of the peppermint schnapps Jones had bought for me in Damascus into my hot chocolate to soothe my cold and aching muscles, and sat on the edge of the shelter with the warm travel mug between my ungloved hands, feeling the heat growing in my palms and belly, promising deep sleep.

The weather the following day came out warm and by the middle of the day was fairly hot. Cain, who we had seen only a couple of times since meeting him in Hot Springs, had spent the night with us the past two nights and was heading home that day. It was a strange thing to see someone getting off the trail, effectively dropping out of existence. But like death it was only grim if a hiker felt he had failed. There had been a great deal of discussion on the trail and among the Vikings about what it meant to hike the trail and what it meant to stop. Squirrelfight intended to hike every inch of the trail, which meant that if we wanted to take a side trail that wound off to the peak of a mountain off the AT and reconnected with the trail a little farther down, he would hike back to where the trails split and then catch back up. He figured that if he was going to go all the way out there to hike the trail, there was no point in missing even one of the white blazes that marked the way. For me, the hike had become its own existence, and anything that happened to me in the course of my travels was a part of the trail experience, whether there were blazes or not, and whether it meant missing a portion of the actual trail or not. Jones thought both ideas sounded good, and was a bit frustrated that there was not a group consensus, but he had a knack for finding a middle way. Our group approach to time was similar. I kept a watch attached to my pack strap and used it to tell how far I had hiked, how long I had before sunset, when the post office would close, and occasionally used it as an early morning alarm. Squirrelfight wanted no watches at all, preferring to live by the natural rhythms of the forest. He wanted to eat when he was hungry and wake when he was rested. As with the hike, Squirrel and I never questioned each other's positions and went on doing it our way, but Jones sought some common ground. After deliberation, he decided to wear a watch so he could track days, dates, and passing time, but set it wrong so he wouldn't be influenced by a preset schedule.

When we came to the road-crossing where Cain hitched to town, we said good-bye to him, wished him well, and spread out in the grass between the dirt road and the woods to eat a lunch of granola, cheese, candy bars, dried fruit, and bagels. It was a late lunch, but we had hiked ten miles already, leaving only a short stretch of five miles to hike after our break. After putting away my food, I stretched out on the grass with my head on my pack to relax in the sun and catch a quick nap. When I opened my eyes, Squirrelfight and Jones were looking at me and grinning slyly.

"Oh, Viking Lord. We've got a plan." Squirrel was beaming.

"What are you guys up to?" I said, half asleep. Jones prepared to illustrate their masterpiece.

"All right. Fourteen more miles today." I winced at the thought, but Jones continued unaffected. "We'll make it to the National Rangers Association. We can sleep on the porch, and there's a phone where we can order pizza." I could see the temptation but wasn't sure if a pizza was worth turning this beautiful day into a grueling drive for miles. Squirrel took up the sword: "But that's not all. That leaves us with only twelve miles left to get to Atkins, which we can do in plenty of time to get a motel room, shower, laundry, and go to the Post Office." Jones chimed in, "And catch *Seinfeld*. It'll be Thursday!" It had been months since I had seen any television and almost as long since I had acknowledged the existence of Thursday night as an important time to watch it. The only reason the days of the week had any bearing on us was because we had to make sure not to arrive at the Post Office on Sunday or too late on Saturday.

"What if we catch up to Scoobie again?"

"Hopefully he really did the twenty-five, and he's in Atkins today. If not, we'll just have to kill him and toss him in a ditch." Squirrelfight grinned.

So much goodness to be had just from hiking a long day after lunch. Such a decisive Viking raid on all the fruits that civilization had to offer! I couldn't argue the genius of the plan, and we set off to hike the rest of that short day turned suddenly so long.

We started together at our well-measured distance: too close and each branch passed would become a whip in the face, too far and we would have to shout to be heard around the pack of the hiker in front. We spoke forward and listened backwards, since the hiker in front would have to stop and turn around to be heard without yelling and we preferred not to break the peace of the forest. We planned out our pizza dinner in a hundred different ways, quoted TV shows we hadn't seen in months, imagined a beautiful farmers' market, and revisited the pizza discussion. As usual, Squirrel and

Jones eventually pulled ahead of me. Squirrelfight was the fastest due to the two magic ski poles he carried. The old white paint was chipping off, but they were sturdy and light. His body twisted back and forth like a tiger with each step. Pushing off with one leg and the other arm, he glided along the trail steadily. Jones hiked fast at times and slower at other times, his rate changing with his moods. He carried a thick wooden stick and each step pushed him as much up as forward. When he was happy he almost bounced, but when anger overtook him he drove along the trail quickly, leaving deep holes from the tip of his staff. Squirrel and I would try to decipher his disposition by reading his staff prints, since his mood could change between one stop and the next. I nearly always fell behind, walking at a stroll and often singing. On long days, when the Vikings would pull into camp around dusk, I would wind in fifteen minutes or so later in the growing darkness. The other Vikings would hear me singing as I came down the trail through the night.

"Blackbird singin' in the dead of night, take these broken wings and learn to fly. All your life, you were only waiting for this moment to arise..."

I knew when I accepted the plan for the long day that I would probably end up doing some night hiking, but I was laying down napping at the time and hadn't considered how weary I would be near the end of those twenty-four when the sun set. By the time I noticed the light dimming, lost in my own thoughts of pizza and a fog of weariness, I wasn't sure how many miles were left or how far ahead the others were. I stopped for a moment before I lost the light and pulled out the map. I hadn't noticed any landmarks for a while, and the rolling hills offered no clue as to where I was. The hiking hadn't been very hard, but my body was aching nonetheless, and I felt unusually tired. Hoping to ease the ache in my neck, back, and legs, I pulled out the half-full bottle of schnapps and took a pull straight from its mouth. With my stomach empty and my blood pumping, the sip had a powerful and immediate effect. As a cascade of relaxation drifted down my muscles, I felt one hundred percent better and hefted my pack to begin walking again.

I glided into the night, not bothering with my headlamp, as the trail had been relatively free of rocks that day. I preferred to walk by the moonlight and follow the trail, which was like a cool black river through the dark trees. I looked hard into the woods ahead, searching for straight horizontal lines, the sure sign of a building, but it was long in coming. I hiked for nearly an hour in the dark, stopping any time the pain would overtake me for another drink of my peppermint potion. I figured I was due for some trail magic about that time. Trail magic was our term for all the little amazing things that happened out on the trail. Sometimes it was as small as finding a Reese's Peanut Butter Cup lying near the trail, still in the wrapper. The week before, Jones and Jokers had found a chilidog lying by a road. It was still warm and pretty clean. Sometimes trail magic was offered by a stranger we met, but often it was left in a place where hikers would find it. The legendary instances of trail magic involved being picked up for a shower, a hot meal, laundry, and a bed to sleep in before being brought back out to the trail. Whatever its measure, trail magic constantly reaffirmed our faith in humanity and the momentum of adventure and reminded us of how wonderfully odd and balanced the world was. Whenever my spirits were low, I would begin to look for trail magic, and usually was not disappointed.

Finally I could see dim lights poking through the darkness. It seemed like I had been toiling in the dark for several hours. The fences and ledges of a government building came into view through the mixed trees, and I made the bird whistle we used to greet each other so as to blend in and not break the harmony of the woods. The reply whistle drifted back as I rounded the last trees. On the wide concrete porch of the building I could see Jones hunched over next to his standard nightly pack explosion, but he wasn't busy setting anything up, and he definitely wasn't eating pizza. At the other end of the porch was another hiker already in his sleeping bag but sitting up against the wall. He was an older man holding a tiny dog and watching the Vikings. Squirrel stood on the side holding a phone, pleading with it.

"You're sure there's nothing you can do? Really? All right, thanks." Squirrel turned away from the phone slowly.

"This sucks," Jones exclaimed, convulsing and knocking over his water bottle. "This really sucks. All day I've been thinking about that pizza. Now I'm so hungry, and this stupid door is locked." I looked behind Jones and saw a locked glass door through which glowed a soda machine and sterile signs marking a bathroom with running water and maybe even showers. The soft drink logo shined through the door like a sadistic beacon.

"They could've at least turned off the lights so it wouldn't look so inviting," I said, realizing as I spoke that my tongue was a little numb. "What's up with the pizza?" I looked over at Squirrel.

"The place that used to deliver out here closed down last week, and the only other place that delivers is Pizza Hut, and they said we're too far."

"In a car?" I tilted my head in disbelief, still feeling minty. "Give me the phone. Call them back." Jones looked up hopefully as I strode imperially over to the phone. Squirrelfight dialed the number again and handed me the phone.

"Hello, Pizza Hut, how can I help you?" A girl's voice crackled over the receiver.

"Hi. This is the Viking Lord. One of my men, Squirrelfight, just called and someone told him that you couldn't deliver any pizza to where we are."

"Yes. That was me. He said you were at the Rangers' Station."

"That's right. There's even a road. I can see it from here."

"Yes sir, but it's outside of our radius. We can deliver to the gas station five miles down the road if you'll just drive down and pick it up."

"Okay, now you listen to me." I was fired up now. "We don't have a car. We hiked twenty-four miles to reach this phone today just so we could have some pizza, and you're telling me that your driver can't push the foot pedal on his car another five miles to save our lives? It's dark, we're too tired to cook, and there's a locked glass door here with glowing bathrooms and soda machines laughing at us on the other side. We're dying out here, and you and your car that won't drive five more miles are killing us." There was a long pause.

"Hold on a second, here's the manager." After a moment there was a shuffling noise and a man's voice came on the line.

"Hi there. You're hiking the trail?"

"Yes, we are." Thank God he knew what the trail was. I could feel the tone shifting. There would be pizza for sure.

"Okay, I'll send someone out there, but you guys had better tip him good."

"On my honor as a Viking." I could hear the manager smile.

I turned to the Vikings. "So did you guys ever decide what you wanted on your pizza?"

Less than an hour later we were eating pizza and laughing again. The weariness of the day sloughed off of us, some of it settling into our legs and heads in anticipation of deep sleep.

"So you finally got your pizza," said the man with the little dog. "Way to go." He had already declined an offer for some of the pizza. He still sat watching while the dog stared wide-eyed at the dripping grease and cheese. In the morning he was gone, and we never saw him again.

CHAPTER 6

Hitching Back to Damascus, Virginia from Daleville
704 miles down and 1,464 miles to go

When I woke up I didn't feel well. We had hiked through some burned-out forest the day before which had bothered my lungs, but it didn't explain the ache in my belly. I didn't say anything about it to the Vikings and let them hike on ahead, but when I finally got myself together and started down the trail, the ache had widened, and dread set in. Was my bleeding ulcer back?

As I undid the straps on my pack to take pressure off my belly, I feared the worst. Pain and anger coursed through me and I dropped my pack to fish out the medications that might save my life. I took the pills without water and moved on to the road nearby with my pack straps open and all the weight on my shoulders. I waited, hunching to a cringing arc when the pain pulsed and sitting on my pack when it subsided, hating my body for trying to destroy itself again. A couple of cars passed me by before I caught a hitch with a chubby guy in a worn out truck. He took me to Daleville where he thought there may be a hospital. The Vikings were hiking to Daleville anyway, though we weren't due to arrive until the next day. Along the way I had two realizations. One was that I actually had an intense case of indigestion, and not a new ulcer. The second was that the driver of the truck was a complete loony. He claimed in the same breath to be on the run from the mafia and to have been switched at birth intentionally by baby traffickers. His story was elaborate and he was pretty convincing, but there was an unsteady way about him that spoke of delusion. I had him drop me at the motel to wait the day and night for Jones and Squirrel as I basked in the relief of not bleeding to death, and checked myself out to be sure I was indeed all right.

When I was checking in and looking over the courtyard, I saw Fly and Aces cleaning off gear with a few other hikers. I hadn't seen the couple since we caught up to them in Damascus, Virginia, a few weeks earlier. We had taken a day off there and fallen behind the couple just as we had in Hot Springs. Now, with 700 miles of trail behind us and two months in the woods, I caught them one last time. I convinced them to wait the night to see Squirrel and Jones, but the next morning when they arrived and we tried to convince Fly and Aces to take the weekend to hitchhike back to the Trail Days Festival with us, we failed. They had to finish in August to make it back to school in the fall. While Squirrelfight and I originally had similar plans, we had both agreed to keep the slower pace we were enjoying even if it meant we wouldn't finish until September or October. A few days earlier at a hostel in Pearisburg, VA, I had called my school to officially withdraw from the coming fall semester. The Viking expedition to Trail Days would take at least three days. Fly and Aces would cover about fifty miles in that time, putting them so far ahead that they would exist only in the registers from then on. Spending the day in Daleville with Fly, Aces, and the others who were hiking on was as much a going away party as anything else. I didn't tell Squirrel and Jones about my stomach. In fact, after all those weeks of being together we knew pretty much everything there was to know about each other, but somehow I never told them about the ulcers which had almost killed me twice in the last three years. I didn't consciously hide it, but despite the terror of the morning that I hitched into Daleville, it remained something that didn't belong with Wayah. Only years later did I realize I had never mentioned it.

Trail Days is an annual festival in celebration of the Appalachian Trail, the people who have finished it in the past, and those who are hiking it that year. It was held in Damascus, though, and we had left that town three weeks earlier. Now, 250 miles away, we would have to hitchhike back. We had planned this, however, and leaving the trail from Daleville was no coincidence. Daleville is a rest stop on I-81, a vein running down the crooked edge of Virginia that would take us straight back to Damascus if we could get an interstate hitch. There were four of us, since one other hiker, Fur Trapper, had decided to hitch with the Vikings. Fur Trapper was another college kid but seemed even younger. He had enough thick black facial hair to rival Squirrelfight, but he had an unmistakable youthful arrogance that peeked out from his testing grin. His trail name was the literal translation of his French surname. It was going to be tough for four grubby men with large bags to get a ride.

We made signs out of the cardboard boxes from our last mail drops, stood in the sun next to the on-ramp, and waited. We had heard that hikers from past years drove down to the festival each year giving rides to hikers so it wouldn't be so hard to get a hitch. Trying to look friendly we each held a sign: "Damascus," "Trail Days," the Appalachian Trail symbol, and the hiker symbol. We did in fact manage to get rides all the way back that day, though we could never fit in one car and arrived at different times.

The town of Damascus crouches over several intersecting streams and rivers just north of the Virginia-Tennessee border, woven together by train bridges, auto bridges, and walking bridges. When we arrived, trickling down the main street in the cars of strangers and new friends, we were confronted by a different kind of horde. In the field between the small town and Laurel Creek, hundreds of tents sat almost on top of each other in tight groupings. The hostel was full and its lawn was also covered with tents. We had been in the woods a long time, but this army had a familiar, comfortable flavor. Circles of people kicked hacky sacs and played instruments in the pockets of grass between the tents. Everyone wore heavy boots with gaiters crawling up their calves or sandals, and they all had pale, wrinkly feet and tan lines around the tops of their ankles. Fleece abounded; scruffy beards and dirty legs were everywhere; and everyone walked the bowlegged, deliberate walk of the worn, chafed hiker—out of the pack and happy. Around the tented field lingered the familiar smell of sun-bleached nylon and stale socks. There were more hikers in Damascus than I had imagined being on the entire trail, and I had a sudden realization of the size of the community to which I belonged.

I had started in mid-March, while the bulk of the people who attempt the entire trail begin in early April. We had always been ahead of the crowd, but here, 250 miles behind us, the masses were lying in siege around Damascus. As happy a gathering as it was, we planned to stay ahead of this mob as long as possible. Most of the hikers had just arrived in town in the last few days, and some had even hitched ahead to make it for the festival. By the time they started to catch up to us, their numbers would be far fewer. Only about ten percent of the people who start the trail actually finish. The vast majority of those drop out by the halfway point, but a startling percentage drop out in the first three days. We predicted that we wouldn't start seeing any of these hikers on the trail until we reached New England. Now and then, hikers would catch up to us, already knowing us all by name and mind from having read our register entries for months. Hikers may have been only a day or so behind, always seeing the Vikings just ahead and imagining our adventures, but to us those hikers didn't exist until they caught up. The gallery of personalities here was the only preview we'd get of the hikers coming up behind.

Looking for a camp away from the circus by the river, known among the hikers as "Tent City," we found an island up-river. It was hidden in the trees and connected to the land by a small bridge. The spot made an excellent Viking camp. We set up our tents in a circle with a space in the middle where we could all sit and cook together. Nearby was a large fire pit, and scattered around the island were several more tents. The ground was loose, sandy dirt, and the tent stakes didn't hold very well, so my tent, which relied on tension from the stakes to stand, was sagging a bit. The others had free-standing tents that were supported by a third pole and only had stakes to keep from blowing away in the wind. All of us enjoyed the soft, cool ground, though. The island was surrounded by the rush of the frigid river, nestled in the shade below the high ridges of the riverbank but just above the water line. It cannot be said enough how soothing the sound of running water outside a tent is. Sleeping comes naturally and restlessness is banished by the rush of the river.

We met and talked with the other inhabitants of the island, and it was mutually decided that they should all become Vikings, that the island would be a Viking Camp and any on it a Viking. The Viking Destroyer constructed a great fire in the pit and newcomers to the island gathered firewood, pledging that for the three days of the festival the fire would never go out. We placed a sign over the bridge to the camp, marking it a Viking Camp, and made torches out of beer cans and lamp oil that we set to flaming on the sides of the sign to light the way through the night. Also staying on the island was the famous Beorn. Beorn was known up and down the trail for many reasons. First of all, he was an enormous man. He stood well over six feet and weighed more than 300 pounds. Second, aside from looking like a giant, he sounded, acted, and drank like a giant. He was known for his high spirits and very loud voice with which he quoted passages from *Romeo and Juliet* whenever there was a woman present. Beorn snored with such volume and tenacity that hikers were known to offer him money to move on when they saw him walking into a shelter.

Beorn was also known for his claims that he was not only hiking the trail, but yo-yoing. He was the only person we had heard declare this besides Scoobie, and everyone had doubts about either of them carrying through.

Being on military disability, Beorn was able to stay on the trail without worrying about his finances, as the checks kept coming in each month, and he could take as much time as he wanted. More recently he was gaining a reputation for excessive yellow-blazing. Hard-core purists on the trail, who claimed that taking even one step off the trail disqualified a hiker from thru-hiker status, were up in arms over Beorn's habits and claims which, admittedly, could be grating at times. The Vikings were not an exclusive group, and our official position on any question related to whether or not someone was hiking correctly was "hike your own hike." With the rush of the river all around us drowning out his snoring, we never had any reason to flee the giant.

That night we met Kaptain Krummholz again, whom we had not seen since Hot Springs, and who had also caught a ride back, but from even farther down the trail. With him was Buzzsaw, a hiker who had always been ahead, but whose register entries were famous, as they were sure to give a laugh. He stepped out of the myth of the trail ahead and over the bridge onto the island. The night soon wrapped us all around the great fire, and we talked and laughed, sharing our stories and adventures and hearing the manifold legends of the trail unfold over us. The trail came before us and passed through us, and anyone and anything on it was our reality. The stories of those ahead illustrated our future and the places and people we would find there, while the stories of those behind lay over the vivid mountains of our past. Some had no knowledge of Vikings, while other hikers knew us well, recalling our register entries and the accounts of people who had met the Horde. We learned that the Pizza Hut near the National Rangers Association now delivered pizza there every night. It was as if we were stepping outside and looking at the world from afar. We stayed up late into the night with laughter and stories, far past our normal hours, knowing that several days would pass before we would get up with the dawn and hike.

The morning was a lazy one. Quiet and rested, we stirred from our tents to the cool rush of the morning river and the wet, blue light of the sunless sky in the steep valley. I gathered those who were awake to the crusty diner on the edge of town to wait and talk for hours while the lone waitress scrambled around the tables, fighting off the hundreds of hikers drooling for a greasy diner breakfast. By noon, our friends from other camps were awake and joined us to walk the fair and see what there was to be plundered. We climbed up out of the shade of the island into the town, where the sun beat hard on the concrete and asphalt. Cars wove around us like ghosts, and all over town, especially where there was food or gear, hikers could be found, moving slowly and blissfully as the outnumbered townsfolk dodged past us on their daily rounds. Through Damascus and past its streets and shops we walked until the town narrowed to one bridge. On the other side was a long thin field lined with stands and carts with food, arts, crafts, and other festive wares. We walked by the crafts, laughing at the thought of buying and carrying one of the baskets or statues which, however flammable, had no place in our lives.

Buying a couple of large plates of onion rings and massive cups of real lemonade, Squirrelfight, Buzzsaw, Fur Trapper, and I walked the crowded main strip of the fair looking for a place to sit and eat. Jones had gone to see about getting his pack fixed, and the Kaptain was nowhere to be found.

"Oh dear," Squirrel said in his sarcastic tone, his attention suddenly fixed far off. I followed the intensity of Squirrel's gaze past the onion rings, through the people walking by to where his eyes played over a truly wondrous sight. She stood by a table some thirty feet away showing a hiker how to juggle, and once I had seen her, I realized that the sun shone more brightly on the grass where her bare feet rested. She stood in a long black skirt and short burgundy top, and when she moved I could see a sliver of her belly, pale and soft and shapely. She had no hiking scars on her hips or feet and a grace and cleanliness that is lost quickly on the trail, but it was her eyes that reminded me of my people in the woods. They sat above her light, easy smile like strips of calm sea as she squinted in the sun.

Women were somewhat rare on the trail. The ratio seemed to be about one woman to every ten men, but most were part of a couple that had started together or met on the trail. There were hundreds of young, single men and a handful of single women, and after two months of hiking, we were becoming tense. After a few more months the tension would crystallize into a painful joke, but in the beginning, women came up in discussion constantly. Being ahead of the crowd, we had met only eight women out of almost ninety hikers, and all of those were unavailable.

"Right," I said finally, "let's sit here." We looked around at the people walking by us and sat down in the middle of the grassy thoroughfare to watch the juggling girl and eat our piles of onion rings. Squirrel had piled catsup on one plate and was smearing it thickly on the rings.

"Have you got enough catsup there, Squirrel?" said Fur Trapper with a chortle, waiting for a response that was slow in coming.

"You can never have too much catsup. This girl is killing me," Squirrel exclaimed in a laughing growl, throwing a packet of catsup on the grass in mock anger. I looked up again and saw her laughing sweetly.

"Why don't you go talk to her?" I said, grinning at Squirrel.

"Yeah, whatever. I'm not that guy," Squirrel said, locking eyes painfully with me. "What would I say?"

"Ask her to show you how to juggle." I nudged my friend. "If you don't, I will."

"I know you will." Squirrel looked back at the juggling girl longingly as I had an amusing moment of reflection. I am very shy, certainly shyer than Squirrel, but Wayah had no need for shyness or the opinions of others, and the Viking Lord had gained a reputation for his boldness. What was this identity game the trail was playing with me? Was I the Wolf, the Viking Lord, or were they both just masks? I was like an audience to my own show, watching myself push farther and farther beyond anything I might have dared before the trail. Now I was trying to get Squirrel to take the same plunge. Squirrelfight was, after all, the Viking Hero. If the girl had been a long drop to a freezing lake, he would have jumped without hesitation. It took several minutes, but Squirrel finally agreed to approach her as soon as the hiker that was talking to her left. The Viking Hero then proceeded to whittle at a small piece of light wood that he had been carrying. Before we knew it, Squirrel was on his feet holding the little wooden ring he had made.

"Well there's my Viking Hero." I leaned back on my hands, genuinely impressed by the gift Squirrel had made and a little jealous of the experience he was about to have. Squirrel approached her with valor and presented his gift as sweetly as she took it. They talked for a little while and then another woman behind the table with the juggling balls got up and angled into the conversation. She looked like she might be the juggling girl's mother, and she moved into a guard position over her daughter. Squirrel tried for a few moments to navigate the conversation before pointing to the rest of us who were watching intently, and the juggling girl turned her enveloping eyes on us. We got up and approached with our sore hiker limps.

"Wayah, Fur Trapper, Buzzsaw, this is Brooke and her mother," Squirrel said, almost relieved. There were scattered introductions and I found myself trapped in Brooke's serene but heavy gaze.

"So are you Vikings also?" she asked, almost taunting. Fur Trapper and Buzzsaw began shaking their heads and explaining their loose affiliation, and I shot them a confused glance before looking back at Brooke.

"Am I a Viking? I'm the Lord of the Vikings."

We invited her to share our fire that night and she brought her younger sister with her. Brooke was young, just in college, and Kelly was in the midst of high school, but they came fearlessly onto the flame-lined isle and brought a drum. That night they stayed only a short while, playing and singing, but we all met again the next day when the rain dampened the festival. We played and sang long into the night, since the next day the festival would end and we would be back on the trail. We parted with embraces, and Brooke gave us her phone number, asking that we call before leaving. When the two girls had gone, Squirrelfight and I looked at each other and breathed deeply, painfully, relieved. I went to my tent soon after to find some long-neglected sleep, and Squirrel and Jones stayed up until the night threatened to become morning, carousing with the others on the island, many of whom we would not meet again.

When I awoke it was certainly morning, but the fabric of my tent was not the bright, patchy spray of light that came with dawn. It was a cool, unlit gray that seemed to grow darker and lighter, churning. I unzipped the tent fly and crawled out, slipping on my boots without lacing them. Stretching in the breeze I saw a sky of the blackest clouds stewing and rolling and speeding across the sky. There were times when such weather would cool things off and blow right over without raining, but there was no reason to risk it and chance having to pack up wet gear. The rest of the island was silent and still, so I warned them of the coming rain in a voice that would wake my comrades enough that they could decide their fate, but not enough to keep them from going back to sleep if they so chose.

The wind pushed around me like a heavy river while I packed up my gear. High in the treetops I could hear violently thrashing branches lashed by high rain and unhindered wind. After rolling and packing my sleeping bag and pad, I pulled up the tent, which had stood loosely on the soft sand for the last three days. I secured all my belongings tightly to the pack, took down my food from where it hung with the other food bags over a branch, and stuffed it in the top pouch. I pulled my rain gear from where it was conveniently stowed for hasty retrieval and fitted the waterproof cover tightly over the pack just as the first heavy drops began to break through the treetops. The others still had not stirred, preferring to take their chances with the rain, but at the sound of the hard drops on his tent, Fur Trapper leapt out, hoping to pack up before anything got too wet. Waterproof, my gear and my person covered and dry, I sat back to watch the rain I loved so much and breathe the wet, cool air. Offering one more chance to escape being drenched, I gave a last call.

"Guys, it's officially raining, and it looks to be picking up," I said in a slightly raised voice to the blank walls of Jones' and Squirrel's tents. A low growl issued from Jones' tent, but Squirrel was all weary defiance.

"I don't care. Let it rain. I'll dry off, but I need to sleep. We just turned in a few hours ago." I took down the other Vikings' food bags from where we had hung a line out of reach of mice and raccoons, and put them in the vestibules of their respective tents so they wouldn't be drenched. The rain came down harder with each passing minute. I could hear Jones inside his tent preparing his gear to be packed and see the sides of the tent shaking with Jones' quick, annoyed movements. It was too late to keep the tent from being thoroughly soaked, and Jones' cursing became audible above the sound of the driving rain. I didn't like packing up wet gear either, since it was heavy and got all the other gear in the pack wet, but Jones took it very hard.

Several other campers on the island were up and about, scurrying to get their gear out of the downpour. We began gathering under a small tarp we set up the day before and talking about setting up a grill for hot dogs when we saw a local woman scurrying over the bridge, wrapped tight in a shiny yellow raincoat. She was upset and calling out, but I had to approach to hear her message over the rain and the rushing water.

"There's a flash flood warning in effect! You all need to get off the island 'cause it goes under water when there's flooding! Everybody needs to get off quick!" I listened to her in disbelief and looked around at the edges of the island, just barely slanting out of the river. The rain poured down harder still. Jones was just coming out of his tent, dismantling it in furious bursts and cursing the soaked nylon, but there was no movement from Squirrel's tent.

"Squirrel! You have to get up!" I shouted through the rain.

"Hell no! Go away and let me sleep! I don't care about the rain!"

"Squirrel! Listen to me! One of the locals just came down and said there's a flood coming and this island is going to be under water! You have to get up now, brother!"

"A flood? Gimme a break!" Almost immediately there was an enormous crash of thunder and the rain doubled its intensity. "Aw, you've got to be kidding me." The sound of Squirrel packing up his gear inside the tent dodged through the rain to my satisfied ear as leaves and branches began hitting the ground with the pounding rain and wind.

"Just get your bag packed and I'll carry your tent up to shelter off the island where you can break it down!" I yelled into the tent amidst Squirrel's muttering. I could tell Squirrel was laughing at himself in exasperated weariness.

"God's playing some sick joke on me! Flood my ass! You've got to be kidding!"

Soon we were scurrying off the island. I carried the unwieldy tent over the bridge and up the stairs to the public pool area where there was an overhang out of the rain. A dozen wet hikers were huddled there with their gear. Squirrel and Jones' eyes were red with weariness, and they sank into concrete corners to attempt sleep. It seemed there wouldn't be much of a fair that day either. We had already arranged a ride back to the trail later that afternoon. Fur Trapper had an uncle nearby who was going that way and offered to give us a ride in his van, all 250 miles back to Daleville where we had hitched off. It was a great relief for us, not to be faced with the prospect of trying to hitchhike all day, wet and smelly. There was still a long day to be spent in the rain, though, waiting for the ride. Since Brooke had left her number, Squirrel and I decided to call her to see if she could get us out of the rain until the afternoon. The thought of seeing her again was a beam of light through the gray clouds.

Tent City was in ruins. We made our way to the pay phone next to the diner through the slowly waning rain past tents filled with several inches of water, their owners laughing or crying. I fumbled through my pocket with wet fingers for a coin and handed it to Squirrel, who dropped it into the slot. The canned, musical tones of the keys bounced through the spattering of the rain. Ringing. And then her soft voice. I watched as Squirrel's face reflected their short conversation and good-bye.

"She'd love to see us again, but she doesn't have a car until later today. If we can get a ride to her house, she'll take us to meet Fur Trapper's uncle. She sounded psyched."

We went to the hostel near the middle of town to find a ride and found another man who was willing to take us all the way back to Daleville, but not fifteen miles the other direction to where Brooke lived. Jones, still weary from the lack of sleep, had been in a foul mood all morning and wasn't interested in Squirrel's and my fascination with Brooke. He decided to take the early ride back to the trail and was gone. The rest of us kept asking drivers around the hostel for a ride and eventually found one. Following the directions she had given us, we wound out of Damascus and soon found ourselves rolling up the drive of a large white house on the top of a hill. The paint was flaking and there was yard-sale debris strewn about the porch, but it was a comfortable, welcoming house, and the rain had stopped. Brooke was soon at the door giving hugs and grinning broadly. We met her father in the kitchen, and then she led us down the stairs in the middle of the house into the basement, which apparently was the domain of her and her sister only. It was a haven for me. Several guitars leaned next to drums, and around the floor and leaning on walls were large pads of paper and charcoal for drawing. Falling into one of the deep couches with a guitar, I felt entirely at peace. I had missed drawing and playing the guitar so much in the past two months, and here were invitations to both in the world of this wonderful, beautiful girl. If only the clock would stop ticking for a while we would have more than a couple of hours, but the time sped by, and Brooke was soon driving us to the truck stop where we were to meet Fur Trapper's uncle.

The sun was shining, and the wet asphalt expanse seemed very empty. I wished for our ride not to come, but as soon as it was wished, Fur Trapper's uncle wound his bus into the parking lot. We packed our gear into the already full van and said good-bye to Brooke one more time.

"You guys could stay with me for a while if you want. I have a friend coming in a week with a bus who could take you back to the trail when he comes through." She asked with a hopeful look in her eyes, mirroring the tone with which we had invited her to our fire two days earlier. I turned to Squirrel, echoing the look.

"What do you say, Squirrel? Are you up for a little more time off?" Squirrel was climbing into the cluttered back of the van.

"The trail's callin', bro. We've been off too long already." Squirrel said.

"Right." I turned to Brooke and hugged her once, then climbed into the front seat and closed the door. As we drove away I caught her eye and saw real disappointment wash over her face, expanding an already empty place in my gut.

The miles rolled by for hours, and I sat pensively entranced. I truly felt I was lost. For the first time I could see another trail that was not along the white blazes. The rolling miles tore me slowly in two. Halfway back to Daleville I looked back at Squirrel in indecision and restlessness. Squirrel was cramped in the back and looked up out of his discomfort.

"Don't look at me! You've got the front seat," he said jokingly.

"I think you'll have the front here in a minute," I said. The words just slipped out, and I realized that I had crossed a line. My stomach quivered a little.

"You're getting out? Are you sure?" Squirrel asked quietly, realizing too where their lines lay and knowing my thoughts like his own.

"You're getting off?" Fur Trapper said in his unencumbered voice that could never whisper. He had just overheard them.

Who's getting off the trail?" Fur Trapper's uncle fired off, looking over the seat.

"I'm not getting off the trail. I'm getting off the bus." It was suddenly done and decided. There was a stillness and quiet, and I sat with a grin, knowing my feet were on the trail again. The van pulled off at the next exit, and they pulled my gear out of the back of the van. Squirrelfight and I grinned at each other, both knowing that we were following our trails as purely as could be done.

"I'll see you next week," I said, the van door slamming shut with everything certain inside it.

"Good luck," said Squirrelfight, grinning.

"You're out of your mind," said Fur Trapper, shaking his head as he climbed back into the bus. His uncle's look echoed his. Fur Trapper's uncle didn't understand why we were on the trail to begin with, and each new detail of our lives simply added to his confusion.

"You know we're taking a few days at Rusty's, so if you haven't caught us by then, we'll see you there, brother," Squirrel said, stretching happily into the front seat.

The bus pulled away with the popping of gravel, and I stood next to the on-ramp entirely alone. Everything I knew for certain rolled away in the bus. My companions, my society, the Appalachian Trail, everything that was familiar was far away now, and all that I had was my own adventure, as unsure as anything. Without the Vikings, there was no Viking Lord. Without the woods, there was no wolf. I stood stripped in the quiet evening, and the earth seemed very large, and every speck of it invaded my senses. I was off the bus and the world was new. It had seemed like such an impossible leap from the other side, but once there was no turning back, I felt utterly calm, and the colors and tastes of that moment were clearer than any other in my life. Each second on the razor's edge dripped with the purest essence of experience.

It occurred to me that Brooke's quick invitation may have been simply polite, or may have been intended only for me and Squirrel together, or even just for Squirrel. I felt doubt in my freedom, but also power. No matter what happened, it was a part of my adventure, and if I had to leave Brooke's porch, embarrassed and awakened from my trance, I would be able to hitch back to the trail again, no matter how long it took, and find my friends. It felt like there was nothing I couldn't do. I began the long hitch back down the highway, and decided that when I got to her town I would stop to call her first and decide then if I was a fool or not. The idea soothed some of my doubts.

We had come a long way from Damascus, and it took many hitches to get all the way back. I got my last hitch just before dark. I told my story to each ride, and some had a hard time believing me about the trail. Some thought me a fool, others a hero, and the last, a chubby Boy Scout leader from Massachusetts, thought I was the only true romantic he had ever met. The thought rang true for me. For what was a romantic but someone who did what felt right to the heart over what was sensible to the mind? It described most everything about my adventure on the trail. The Scout leader was enjoying my stories so much that he decided to go out of his way and take me straight to her town, then asked how to get to the house. It occurred to me as I pulled up to the white house for the second time that I would not get to make my phone call, and my reckoning would indeed come right there on that cluttered porch that suddenly didn't seem so safe. The Scout leader wished me luck, and pulled his tan truck out of the drive, turning on his lights as he faced into the dusk.

I slung my pack over my shoulder and looked down the hill, wondering if I was going to have to hike down that road tonight. I pocketed my doubts and turned to the house. I heard the whisper of the Wolf, the boom of the Viking Lord. If this was my trail, what place on it was not the woods, and who along the way was not a Viking? I felt strong and sure, and approached the door as if the next blaze were brushed on its side. It was open, and through it I saw into the kitchen where she stood, talking to her father. She seemed so light, so unencumbered, and I knocked on the old wooden frame of the door. She looked up from her conversation and stood for a moment, frozen, then came smiling toward the door, pushing off every few steps to glide along a little faster. As she opened the door, I could see her eyes, and they shone in perfect joy and reflected my happiness. I was no fool after all, and I felt invincible. I had shed everything that was sure and known for this moment and past it all I found warm affirmation. I held her and she melted softly into me.

The next three days were half restful dream and half negotiation. I determined to convince Brooke to join me on the AT, but she didn't have any ambition for such a journey and after carrying around the full pack for a bit, thought she would just slow me down anyway. I tried to think of ways that we could join in an adventure together, but she couldn't imagine shedding her surroundings the way I had done. Having just made that jump, I knew how frightening it was, but had assumed that she would jump right in the way other details of my adventure seemed to fall into place. As the days went by I realized that my reward was not a life with Brooke, but discovering that I was more than my surroundings. I had gotten off the bus and found my own power in the void. In the end, Brooke and her father drove me over the long miles back to the trail, and we parted with another brief embrace. I turned back to the woods, smelling oddly of soap and shampoo, my clothes cleaner than any day since I started, and leaned back into the forest, gathering strength to begin the long task of catching up to my friends. My pack felt heavier, and there was sadness on me, but I carried a new vigor, and a set of handmade juggling balls.

Interlude at Rusty's

On nights when Northmen ride the wind
Those hearty, strong, and able men
Past river wide and mountains high
Where weary sleep and blistered cry
To camps and unsuspecting hosts
On guard to all of woodland ghosts
'Tis wise to watch with keenest eye
And listen quick with axe nearby
For Vikings may be laughing friends
But by their wrath might meet your end.

It was on such a night as this
That Vikings strode out of the mist
And up to gas-lit hall they slid
Where Rusty's Hard Time crew were hid
Sat two in front that caught the sight
Of warrior boots astride the night
Leaped one from stool and one from chair
Called "I'm Spicoli, who goes there?"
And Wayah, Jones, and Squirrelfight cheer
"All hail the Vikings! Foes to fear!"

From darkest corner out of view
Spicoli pulled and great horn drew
And grinning at his newfound foes
Crying peals of mighty blows
And from the darkest sleeping hall
The host with glee poured o'er the wall
Now two turned twelve to Viking three
And rested were their enemy
When up arose a belly roar,
Stood Rusty at the Hollow's door.

He sauntered forth with hefty grin
A wily beard and glasses thin
And held on high a camera flash
That lit the meadow, lightning splash

And when the blasting light had thinned
Their picture on the roof was pinned
And striding to them without fear
He laughed and pulled out six cold beers
Said, "Gruff though they are to the eye
I've heard of these from hikers-bye.

"These Vikings though they play at fright
Share their cookfires every night
And weary hikers, losing faith
Have laughed with them till bellies ached
And finding joy in climbing rocks
Found happiness that they had lost
So look you past their warrior stance
And welcome tired friends to dance!
Spicoli! Bring the truck around
And open doors for my James Brown!"

On the truck's high platform then
Climbed Vikings all and Hollow men
And laughed and danced with lifted mood
And cried to heaven "I feel good!"
The truck did lean and bounce around
And past the night there echoed sound
Of hiker paradise they found
When came the Horde to Rusty's ground
Through many days of rest they stayed
And long-time friends among them made.

Many of you hear and wonder
Where you might procure such plunder
When townsfolk do not understand
The rowdy longings of your band
You seek the house where Rusty's King
And put on your decoder ring
For Hollow's closed to those outside
The hikers for a place to hide
Instead of looking back and forth
Just go to Springer, then hike north.

CHAPTER 7

Hightop Hut, Shenandoah National Park, Virginia
873 miles down and 1,293 miles to go

Pine Swamp Branch Shelter:
*An ostrich my foot!! There are no ostrich out here –
everyone knows that. Anyone gullible enough to believe
such a 'tall' neck of a story ought to be in a padded cell.
As for those who write such baloney—straightjacket time!*

*We had a good days hike from the campsite four miles
out of Pearisburg, although suffering from too much town
food and bugs. Oh yes, we saw an elephant today
(seriously) flying high, circling the turkey vultures before
diving down into the bushes to gobble up some
unsuspecting peanut hiking to Maine.*

Sulu - the third Brit
GA > ME

*When did the National Park Service start the Ostrich
relocation program in Central Virginia?*

Blind Owl
GA > ME

"Now there are a lot of bears in the park," said the
Ranger, "and you're bound to run into one on your way
through." The Ranger had cornered me and Squirrelfight
as we stopped to fill out our back country permits for the
Shenandoah National Park. In large capital letters across
the entire permit where you were supposed to record
vital information and schedules we had written
"VIKINGS."

"Now if a bear should charge you, just hold your ground 'cause it's probably a false charge and he'll turn away at the last second." I glanced over at Squirrelfight and saw him intently visualizing the encounter. There was a leaf stuck in his dread locks. "Now if he should get up to you, just drop down and ball up. He might mess up your pack, but he probably won't do more than bat you around." The Ranger was starting to sound like a safety pamphlet, and after the thought of standing up to a charging bear had run its course, we began looking for an appropriate exit. "On the other hand," continued the Ranger, "if a bobcat should come after you, you've got no way out but to beat the hell out of it, cause they just won't stop until you're dead." I looked back at Squirrelfight with a gleam in my eye. His face was already animated with excitement.

"Oh, man!" Squirrelfight yelled, somewhere between laughter and epiphany. "I hope I get attacked by a bobcat!" He started flailing around the road, punching the air and strangling some unfortunate imaginary bobcat that just happened to be in the wrong place at the wrong time. I started laughing and stretched my arms out in front of me.

"Imagine the scars you would have after that scrap! 'Yeah, well you should see the bobcat!'" I emerged from our fantasy to find the Ranger staring concerned, perhaps even frightened. It occurred to me that the lawman might decide to have us put away, locked in some treeless cell without ice cream. No way, the Ranger didn't have a chance. We outnumbered him, and Squirrelfight already had the blood of one imaginary bobcat in his teeth today.

"Don't worry about us, tough guy," I said, suddenly a little confrontational. Squirrelfight's face was still red with laughter and every now and then he would cry out and kick the ravaged bobcat across the road.

Striking out into the Shenandoah, we were about 100 miles from Harpers Ferry, West Virginia, the 1,000 mile mark and spiritual midway point on the trail. It was just the two of us since Jones had hiked out of Rusty's with another group a couple of days before we left and Fur Trapper, who had remained with the Vikings since Trail Days, met his parents in the first days of hiking the Shenandoah to go home for a short break. Jones had become more and more tense in the last month and would become exasperated with me and Squirrel's easiness with the trials that tormented him. I didn't know if we'd see him again or not, but he definitely needed a break from us. His desire to complete the trail was eclipsing the joy of hiking it, and each time we indulged in our experience, he would become agitated. Now Squirrelfight was planning to get off at Harpers Ferry for a week to go to his sister's wedding. I had no such break in store and no thoughts about the future other than to enjoy my friend for these hundred miles before he left.

Squirrelfight had planned his departure so that he would have hiked 1,000 miles before he went home. We had counted the miles for a long time. The first 100 miles was a victory, as was the second, but after a while, another 100 miles was something to be noted but not necessarily celebrated. One thousand miles. It's the kind of thing you joke about or write songs about, but we were about to have hiked it. It wasn't quite halfway, but to have hiked a thousand miles over the mountains was to cross into the unquantifiable. The mind simply can't hold on to 1,000 miles, or the difference between 1,000 miles and 1,200 miles. In a sense, a day's hike no longer added noticeably to the whole, but the counting up had ended and the counting down began. We were moving forward, having the time of our lives, and we began looking far to the North where Katahdin could now be felt and hunted.

Squirrelfight's birthday was the day after Memorial Day. He would be twenty-four, and looking at his map we could see a shelter exactly twenty-four miles away. I thought it would be better to take it easy and relax on Squirrel's birthday, but since Squirrel was so clearly excited about doing twenty-four for his twenty-fourth, I consented to the miles.

The day was a beauty, and we walked some together and some alone all morning. We were dipping through lush green valleys and crisscrossing Skyline Drive, the road that slices through the trees for the length of the Shenandoah Mountains. We passed outcroppings and wide spaces in the road where drivers could pull over and look through their car windows and across the guardrails to the world we called home. The trail was accessible by road all through the National Park, which had good points and bad ones. On the bad side, hikers were vulnerable to casual crime and pestering drivers, not to mention the mental impact of constantly hearing the passing cars. It was bad enough having to see and cross the road now and then without having to always know the road was nearby. Squirrel stopped to piss on the yellow line in the middle. On the good side, the enormous campgrounds were usually full of RVs and tents and people with too much food and a willingness to give it to tired, sweaty, starving thru-hikers. The art of bumming food from townsfolk was affectionately referred to as "yogiing." The only rule for this hiker sport was that one could never directly ask for anything. Even hinting was considered poor form. The weekenders and locals had to be coaxed into offering their various treasures and still think it was their own idea. In North Carolina, I had met a south-bounder (a thru-hiker starting in Maine and going south) named Knothole Willie. Willie had shared his favorite yogi with the rest of the hikers around the fire that night. He would sit near a group that was out picnicking, and while answering questions about the trail, he would spend minutes scraping the inside of an empty peanut butter jar with his spoon, smudging tiny particles of peanut butter onto a mangled piece of bread, letting the bread rip and crumble under the dry spoon. They would always feel so sorry for him that they would invite him to join their meal. Stories of the trail are filled with these hopeful transactions, even those that were less than successful.

Hemlock Hill Shelter
Nice to see Fly and Aces here at the shelter when I arrived. Last night when I arrived at Crampton Gap Shelter, there were two people having chicken right there on the front step of the shelter, and we're not talking Buffalo chicken wings here, these two were having the all-you-can-eat BUFFET. They paid no attention to me when I arrived and continued marinating each other (I mean the chicken), so I made it clear that I was there to stay by laying out my Thermarest pad and then hanging my REEKING socks directly over their heads. After a few minutes, the grill cooled down, and they left, disgruntled. Is it possible to be gruntled?
-the thru-hiker formerly known as Buzzsaw
GA>ME

It was Memorial Day weekend in the National Park, normally a yogiing paradise, but after a few days of heavy rain, the park was nearly empty. We stood in the ruin of a car camping lot over the moistened remains of red, white, and blue paper ribbon and flag-colored paper hats, wondering if the camp store was open. I left my pack with Squirrelfight and went to scout out the store, finding it open and stocked with goodies more than adequate for a birthday lunch. I brought back two cokes, a half gallon of ice cream, a dish of fudge, and six beers. We sat in the shade of the moist canopy eating and drinking, then threw the containers in one of the trashcans, along with our pack trash of the last few days and kept hiking. We climbed and hiked at a relaxed but steady pace, taking long breaks at the tops of mountains or to do a little scrambling off the trail on a separate peak.

Viking Rule: We stand on big rocks

We leaped from boulder to boulder along the cresting ridges near the trail, and sent barbaric yawps back and forth over the expanses of trees and the long, deep-swept landscape with the road cutting always somewhere far below us. The day skipped along slowly under us and around us, and it became obvious that we were going to have to do some hiking in the dark to make the twenty-four miles that day since we were traveling at a leisurely pace. We had made a lazy start of the day and never found a reason to hurry. The air was cool in the wake of the rains, and we were enjoying the perfect embrace of Squirrel's long birthday hike. Squirrelfight had always been the slowest getting ready in the morning. In the first months the rest of us would wait for him to get himself together and stretch after breakfast every morning. Often, just as we thought he was ready, he'd put everything down again and say "Time for my morning movement! If I put my pack around this belly I'll poop my pants." Of late we had taken to leaving him, knowing he would catch up with his magic poles. On his birthday, though, I waited for him, and Squirrel took a pace more like mine so that we hiked together almost all day. I even took web-catcher position when we started the morning, hiking out in front with my stick bobbing up and down to clear out the spiders' efforts of the night.

Looking at the map, I wondered where we would be at nightfall. There was a restaurant/bar on the trail several miles ahead at a resort by the road. It would be dark when we got there, but the guidebooks indicated that it would be open late so we decided to raid it and continue the celebration there before pushing on the last few miles in the dark to the shelter.

Night fell on us quickly and it was darker than usual, only two days after the new moon. We stumbled along the rocky trail, looking for a light through the trees. Squirrel's lamp was dying, and when we stopped to replace the battery, he found that the spare had melted somewhere along the way. We had to move slowly with only one headlamp, the light casting sharp and deceptive shadows that made it hard for Squirrelfight to find his footing behind me. The miles crept by for what seemed like hours before we began to see specks of light through the trees on the right. We passed the huts and bungalows of the resort for a good stretch before coming to a splinter path with a post marking the way to the restaurant. We carried our packs up the ridge and into cones of street lamps that lit paved paths among the buildings, finally coming to a wide lawn in front of the main lounge of the resort. The light from inside the glass door bled like a sterile wipe over the sign reading "No Packs." It was common in touristy places near the trail to forbid packs indoors. Truthfully a collection of hikers in an enclosed area generated quite a smell, but it was clearly a kind of segregation meaning "if you come in, don't stay long."

We found a clump of manicured bushes in a dark corner and stashed the packs among them before going to the door and pushing it open. The blast of cold artificial air littered with traces of lounge music and the carpet under our feet made us grin. We were tired, but there would be a great deal to plunder here. We followed the noise through the luxury-cluttered lounge and down a set of stairs to the basement. We limped past the clean white walls and glass doors into a dark room with red ornamental carpets and small round tables. Couples and groups were huddled over the tables or reclined around them, and every one turned and watched us saunter across the room. The hiker limp is a noble swagger. The legs are fatigued, the feet are sore, and there is usually some chafing in the nether regions to add a little "Fred Sanford" to the swing, but the body is free of the strain of the pack and stretches and twists freely.

The clean, freshly showered and laundered patrons looked uncomfortable as Squirrelfight and I walked by— as if we were pan-handlers or bums that would look over all their wealth and style and beg feebly for a piece of it.

Their fear was amusing, but we were too tired for nonsense and made our way to the bar, annexing two stools with soft, cushioned tops.

"A.T. hikers? What can I get you to drink?" asked a smiling lady behind the bar. She had a kind face, just starting to age. I ordered a beer, and Squirrel the whisky he loved so well.

"What we really need, though, is some food," said Squirrelfight, his stomach groaning.

"Oh, the kitchen just closed a little while ago." She seemed genuinely sorry. I looked around the room at large plates with pieces of pizza, chicken, sandwiches, and steaks with only a few bites taken out of them and napkins and silverware strewn on top, begging retrieval.

"How about when you throw away all those people's food you could accidentally drop it all in a big bowl for us? We'll be very discreet." Her eyes opened in profound sympathy, but then she squinted and shook her head. "Oh well," I said, too tired to push it farther and enjoying feeling my muscles beginning to relax from the drink, as the bartender disappeared in the back. "A very happy birthday, my friend," I toasted Squirrel, "and an excellent day."

"Indeed," said Squirrel, swallowing his drink. From around the corner came the bartender, holding a large plate of fruit and two bags of chips.

"I managed to scrounge this stuff up from the kitchen."

"Thank you so much," I said. "You're a life-saver." The fruit plate wasn't dinner, but it would hold off our hunger for a while until we went back outside to cook some food. The fresh fruit really hit the spot, though, and the gentle touch of trail magic swelled our hearts.

"Did I hear you say it was somebody's birthday?" the bartender asked, still on a gift-giving high. We nodded, and I pointed to Squirrelfight. "Well, I guess I'd better buy you a drink." There was a warm light between the three of us. I had decided long ago to accept any gift that a person offered me, whether I needed it or not. Some people could sense the adventure we were having, and it excited a part of them that longed for adventure but couldn't escape. They wanted to contribute and put a piece of themselves into it. To turn their gifts down seemed cruel.

We sat at the bar, talking, eating fruit, and enjoying our new friend for a good while before going back out into the hall where there were a pair of phones. We called friends and family, sharing our high spirits with faraway people living in another world. There was a large, open closet down the hall past the phones with maintenance gear and a comfortable couch, and we took shifts lying on the couch or using the phone. We half expected someone to come back to lock up the closet, but through long phone conversations no one came. It was already midnight, several hours after we were normally asleep, and the couch was comfortable and inviting.

"So, do you think we should call it a night here?" Squirrel asked, sizing up the maintenance room as a hideout and sensing my weariness. I looked up at him from the softness of the couch. My body was crying for sleep, and Squirrel seemed willing to cut the day short of his goal. Sublime rest could be mine with a word, but at the sight of Squirrel's resignation the first words out of my mouth were those of the Viking Lord.

"What kind of talk is that?" I said, hoisting myself up on one elbow. "We've still got four miles to hike." A huge grin leaped to Squirrel's face.

"Right on."

We went outside to collect our packs, and sat cross-legged, cooking a proper dinner of mac n' cheese with tuna fish under the light of one of the path lamps. By the time we started hiking it was past one. We stumbled over the rocky trail, tripping on roots and trying to make my light work for both of us. It was a long stretch of hours in the blackness with the one dancing beam of light throwing a strobe of shadows around us. We came to the shelter in a clearing where the starlight and sliver of moon could barely hold to the ground, and we tried to be quiet enough not to wake the hikers that were curled up inside as we climbed in and prepared for a much deserved sleep.

"Thanks, Wayah," came Squirrelfight's whisper from the dark corner of the shelter.

"Happy Birthday," I replied.

"You guys better be Thru-hikers," came a groan from one of the sleeping bags.

"The Vikings are upon you," I whispered into the dark. The dim stars lit the ground in the clearing outside the shelter with a quiet deep blue and crickets called to each other through the slight moonlight and the moisture of a day close to breaking.

Days before, when the Vikings were all together, we had made a list. Squirrelfight loved to make lists, and this one was a list of hiker trail names that you would never hear on the Appalachian Trail. We had laughed a lot trying to think of things that no one would want to be called: Privy Dunker, Crawling Bleeding Guy, Bag Wetter, and so on. Now as we walked through the Shenandoahs, we traded laughter back and forth, making up new names and stories to go with them. When we reached a shelter in the middle of the day, Squirrelfight and I sat down to write a fictitious entry for one of the characters we had created. Through our discussion, I had come up with a way to write it so that it would sound more believable, assuming no one recognized my handwriting. Giggling to myself I began my entry.

Hightop Hut
I enjoyed the privy at the last shelter. I think if Weathercarrot had looked more closely, it might have made his list. Apparently I forgot to lock the door, though, and I had an interesting run-in with Squirrelfight. He must have been pretty embarrassed, and when I got out, he

even seemed upset, so I just left. I think he was yelling at
me as I went. Can't we all just get along?

-The Privy Dunker

Then Squirrelfight sat down to sculpt his reply, marked as the next day.

I can't believe this guy. Let me explain about the 'interesting run-in' we had. I got to Pass-Mountain Hut and had to use the privy real bad. I ran in there, jumped on the seat and started going. Suddenly I heard a moan from underneath and a gloved hand touched my ass! This guy was under the seat! I never moved so fast in all my life. Damn right I was upset! This guy comes crawling out a few minutes later wearing these weirdo gaiters looking like some kind of freaked out fly fisherman with crap all over him. This guy traumatized me big time, man. I have to go right now but I'm not going in any privies for a while... I hope you never meet the Privy Dunker, and I'd better not see him again.

-Seeking Therapy
Squirrelfight

We sat on the wooden bench in front of the empty Hightop Hut, laughing uncontrollably. We were tucked under the overhanging roof out of the sun taking a break from the heat while giving birth to the Privy Dunker, who, as far as the hikers behind us knew, now stalked the woods somewhere ahead.

"Nirvana," Squirrel said between laughs, and I glanced around out of the corner of my eye to avoid arousing suspicion. The code used to be "Have you heard of that band Nirvana?" meaning that one of us saw strangers coming. We would just insert it in our conversation and then continue on, aware that we were not alone. After a while we shortened it for easier insertion. It's not that we were saying anything confidential, only that dealing with non-hikers required some mental preparation, and we could pass for civilized if we weren't surprised.

From the trail that led to the road, a man and a woman wearing matching red T-shirts bounced up to the table by the shelter. They looked like the sort of people who existed to be someone else's wacky neighbors. The man had a bad hat, and they both had cameras. When they saw us, they giggled and stopped where they were, grinning like cows out of the pen.

"Is it all right if we come down here?" the woman asked. "We don't mean to disturb you." I shrugged in mid-laugh, but Squirrelfight was still laughing too hard to acknowledge them. The couple commenced taking pictures of everything on the premises, asking our permission if their subject included us or our gear. Further into their roll they became bolder and started to venture outside the camp area. "Could you tell me where the spring is? I want to snap a picture of it."

"Sure," I said, "just follow the arrow over there with 'spring' painted on it." Squirrel was emerging from laughter into a heavy gasping stage after re-reading the entries.

We hiked on into the afternoon, ascending the ridge and then hearing the road on the other side of it. At an intersection in the trail there was a small wooden sign reading, "Scenic view." The white blazes went off the other way.

"Let's check it out," Squirrel suggested. "We'll leave the packs here." I unclasped the belt of my pack and let it slide down my back and legs until it rested on the ground. It had a free-standing external frame and I leaned it up against a tree, unzipped the main pouch and pulled out my snack bag. Squirrel swung his pack from his shoulder to his knee before putting it down to rifle through the gear on top for his snacks. He laid it on the ground next to mine and pulled one of his water bottles from where it was nestled on the outside of the pack. I also grabbed one of my water bottles and we headed down the short trail. It emerged onto some rocks and we climbed over the boulders to where the rocks dropped off sheer down to the road, where cars were pulling over to see the view over the rail, and down into a deep valley. We looked over the steady, mild slopes of the Shenandoah for a while, and began watching the cars go by. No one saw us perched among the rocks above, and Squirrelfight started tossing M&M's down the cliff face at them. We hadn't been wanting for food as much lately, since we were moving faster between re-supply points and the intensifying heat had curbed our hunger a bit. In the past months he would never have spared the M&M's. He would have eaten them off the ground if he had been lucky enough to find any.

"None of them get out or even stop," said Squirrel. "They just slow down on the gravel pull-off near the rail and then speed back up and go on. What do they think they're seeing?"

"I guess a glimpse through sunglasses and tinted windows and air conditioning is better than nothing." Squirrel stood up and sounded his barbaric yawp to the sight and smell and feel and taste and life of the land, and another car rolled slowly by.

CHAPTER 8

232 miles across Pennsylvania to Delaware Water Gap
1,265 miles down and 903 miles to go

Pinefield Hut:
For those of you who think that hiking the Appalachian Trail is not a competition, I'd like to inform you that you're wrong. It isn't a RACE, and it's not a contest for the most yellow-blazes, worst flatulence, loudest snore, most inarticulate entries, or most alternative trail names - but it is a competition. And even if you abhor competition, you've entered as of the moment you strode past your first white blaze. And I'm WINNING. I'd tell you what the competition is, but I don't want to give up my advantage.

Buzzsaw
GA > ME

Charles Ferry Shelter:
That's right - you heard 'em. WET! It's so wet my bones are soggy. It's so wet that all I have to do when I'm thirsty is shake a tree. The Susquehanna has risen 2/3 of the way up the mountain, so I hardly even had to climb to get here. Well, I'm gonna swim on over to the next shelter since it's up higher and the river is gaining ground.

Kaptain Krummholz
GA > ME

P. S. Howdy (Recently outlawed word) to Fur Trapper, Wayah, Squirrelfight, and Jones (who I thought I'd be seeing soon but seem to have missed). Hope to see y'all (Recently outlawed word) soon.

I was in a peculiar predicament. I had stayed a little while in Harpers Ferry, West Virginia, after Squirrelfight went home for a week so that it would be easier for him to catch up when he got back on. I had hoped to reunite with Jones, but instead I found his walking stick in town and thought it strange that he would leave it. Jones had carried the thick staff since before we met and had carved the Appalachian Trail symbol into the top of it. He had even kept it after the end cracked, holding it fast with duct tape. When I walked into the Appalachian Trail Conference Headquarters, though, there it was with the discarded walking sticks, the unmistakable duct tape frayed and gashed and the haft dark and smooth from oil and sweat. I just stared at it for a while before Wayah, the Viking Lord, and Tanner all agreed on what I was seeing. Whenever I reached a larger town, Tanner tended to emerge. Between driver's licenses, phone calls, restaurants, and townsfolk, my newer masks would begin to give way, and the old would emerge. It had happened less and less as the trail pushed on, but Harper's Ferry was a metropolis compared to most trail towns, and this conundrum with Jones' stick required as many heads as possible. It was possible Jones had actually grown tired of the weakening stick and discarded it, but it seemed unlikely.

The next day when I was collecting my own mail drop, a package arrived for Jones and I quickly decided to next-day mail the heavy box to Jones' next stop. He had clearly been here and clearly left without it. If he had just blazed through, I hoped it would beat him to his next stop. If he had given up on the trail, then it wouldn't matter to him anyway. I hadn't seen Jones since the Viking Destroyer left Rusty's before the rest of us. He had been down, irritable, and moody, and I had to consider that he may have decided that half of the trail was enough. I left Harpers Ferry unsure and feeling distant from the Vikings. I hiked a normal pace, hoping to catch Jones if he was ahead, but not wanting to put too many miles on before Squirrel got back. Not until I was crossing over from Maryland into Pennsylvania, passing the fabled Mason-Dixon Line, did I catch Dr. DooRiddle, one of the hikers Jones had left Rusty's with. He told me that Jones had gotten off the trail for a week due to a death in the family. Suddenly I was in front, and quite a ways in front. I had four days' lead on both Jones and Squirrelfight, almost 60 miles, and they would be hard-pressed to catch up. I felt very peaceful at home with myself in the woods, but my friends were my family and my community, and I was eager for their return. If I hiked at a normal pace it might be months before I saw them again, and they would probably give up on catching me.

So I hiked as slowly as I could. I couldn't just stop and wait for the Vikings because I would run out of food. My mail drops were already sent and waiting in post offices ahead. All I could do was stretch my food and move as slowly as hunger would allow. I took my time, rarely hiking more than ten miles a day. Pennsylvania was, in the beginning, some of the easiest, most level trail to that point. Hiking for only three or four hours a day, I had a lot of spare time. The trail ran up onto low ridges and stayed on them for long stretches before dropping down to the dry valleys. Often the trail would run through and between fields of wheat or corn. The hiking was leisurely, but the heat was coming on. The long stretches across open fields in the blazing sun reminded me how much the trees protected us even on the hottest days. I would check every side trail, stop at every view, climb any rocks, and nap in the shade. When it looked like rain I would sit under an out-cropping and read *Siddhartha* again. The days were lazy and lonely. There were other hikers, more in fact than usual, but most had started in Harpers Ferry, and the few thru-hikers to be found were strangers from behind going faster and disappearing quickly. They knew my name, but were surprised to hear that I was the Viking Lord, expecting to see me surrounded by dozens of Viking axe-men. I was amused to find that many people were unsure of the size of the horde, but for now I was the Wolf, traveling alone until my fellows caught up.

The trails were more crowded with summer hikers, section hikers starting at the halfway point, and general day hikers. I hiked with Kit Kat through open, flat fields during her last days on the trail before she got off in Duncannon, and I spent a day with a guitar player who had isolated himself in the woods to quit smoking, but most days I would hike alone. I would camp near the new hikers, talking and helping and laughing with them, but their laughter wasn't as easy, they didn't sit down to pot-luck, and it was at dinner that I felt alone.

I strode serenely out of the wet trees into a moist clearing. The grass was still glistening from some light rain earlier in the day, and the toes of my boots were darkened from the water whipping off the grass. The boot leather had once been black but now was a weathered, cracked gray. Squirrel's soles had come off just before he went home, and I wondered how much longer my own boots would hold out. With over 1,000 miles underfoot they were going strong, but the leather around the toes and sides had many little and a few large slashes from every rock I had kicked or tripped over, and the edges of the soles were threatening to separate.

There were two small lean-tos that looked more like scale models than shelters. I walked to the first one and looked around the inside. It was a typical, if strangely small, shelter. There were empty food bag hangers jutting from the overhanging roof, a pair of old socks someone had left in the corner, and nailed to the left wall was a metal box with a flap on it. I flipped open the lid and pulled out the tattered spiral notebook with "Birch Run Shelter Register" scrawled on the front with a magic marker. Leaning my pack against the lip of the sleeping platform, I sat down and read. The register belonged to someone I didn't know. Inside the front cover a message asked that the notebook be returned to the owner when it was full and offered a reward to the person who did (a common practice). It would be quite a souvenir to have one of these registers with the thoughts and comments of so many hikers, known or otherwise. Some hikers carried a blank notebook with them in case they came to a shelter with no register or a full one so they could leave their own.

I flipped through the book, stopping to read the entries of hikers I knew or those who had written humorous entries in the past and to glance over the rest since I had the time. This register was dominated by a discussion of what gear one did or didn't need on the trail. Such discussions were common, often arguments between the same groups of people who would likely never meet each other. Arguments over purist ideology or what it meant to be a thru-hiker seemed to rage endlessly. They gave the Vikings a chuckle. "Hike your own hike." How many times had we heard it? It didn't matter to those arguing, though, so I found it best to poke fun. I remembered a time in Virginia when Squirrelfight and I were on a ridge and needed water. There was a path to a spring, but it went straight down the sheer wall of the ridge. We decided to leave our packs at the top, bringing only our water bottles. Squirrel had joked that if our packs were stolen we could continue hiking down the trail with our water bottles saying to everyone we met that anyone who needed more than a water bottle, a pair of boots, and a pair of shorts had no business being on the trail. I took the chewed cap off the ballpoint pen that was hanging from the register and wrote my entry, wondering when Squirrel would read it.

Came in last night after a whopping 7 1/2 mile day. Of course, with my new Viking powers I made it in eleven minutes. I read Siddhartha *yesterday. It's filled with great wisdom, none of which I will impart here.*

I sent all my gear home from South Mountain. I now have a pair of shorts (for diplomatic reasons), one nalgene, and an axe. Anyone who carries more than that is a wimp. Actually, I may pick up another axe, perhaps

even a flaming brand, but that's all! Anyone who can't live
with this equipment and maybe an oven mitt should just
go home.

Wayah the Wolf
Viking Lord
GA > ME

I kept on as slowly as I could bear with the dry and increasingly rocky terrain of Pennsylvania an unrewarding landscape. The days were hot, and it seemed the trees kept out the breeze, and the ridges were never high enough to break out of them. When the trees did break, I would look out, expecting to see a refreshing vista, but instead see a gash in the earth making way for sets of power lines riding up and down the mountain, buzzing with disharmony. One hot morning I rose early and excited. Looking over the data book, I planned out what would hopefully be the last of my short days. By my calculations it was time to see the Vikings again, who were surely traveling together by now, having returned to the trail within a couple of days of each other. I should have ended up with about an eighty-mile lead on them and with my short days, if they did fifteen-eighteen milers each day they should catch up about now. Less than ten miles away was the town of Port Clinton. I would make my way there at a leisurely pace and then eat in the restaurant and prepare to celebrate our reunion. Even if they didn't arrive today, I could wait through the next day and surely they would arrive by then. I scribbled my plan into the shelter register, "cameled up" (filtered and drank a quart) and filled both my water bottles since some of the water sources had been dry and there was only one water source listed over the ten-mile stretch, and even that was marked as a few tenths off the trail.

I hiked out at a relaxed pace. After more than three months on my feet I could feel my speed pretty accurately. Some days when I was killing time I would hike at a two mile-per-hour pace, similar to a normal pace for an uphill climb, but today I walked closer to three since my pack was empty, water could be hard to come by, and at that pace I could have a greasy burger for lunch in less than four hours. I strode along, my attention turned mostly inward. I was thinking about the Vikings, remembering our laughter and the way we always supported each other, planned our meals together, and filled in the gaps where each one of us left off. I remembered when one of my mail drops wasn't at the post office how we bought whatever we could stomach from a dingy little gas station and then rationed out and shared everyone's food so that we all had mostly good food, and hiked faster so we wouldn't go hungry. I remembered when Squirrel got poison ivy on the bottoms of his feet and they blistered and peeled off, how Jones tenderly made a cast of tape to keep them compressed and we shared his weight and moved slowly, keeping him laughing when his body was screaming. After months on the trail I had learned to deal with many kinds of hardship and have perspective on the fleeting discomforts, but we had taught each other, reminded each other, and supported each other.

I sat down to eat the last of my food, some gorp and peanut butter. Looking at my watch I calculated that I had gone about seven miles. On the elevation profile I could see a steep drop just before town, which was common. Towns are mostly built around rivers, so you usually drop down into them. I saved a few sips of water for the last mile and headed down the trail, looking outwardly now. It was a sunny day, milder than some, hotter than most, but my pack was very light, out of food and water and not carrying my cold weather gear any more. The landscape was mild, rolling, yellow-green, and I bounded along, looking for the big downhill slope that would lead into town. After a while I glanced down at my watch again with a little confusion. A mile takes about twenty minutes at that pace, and it had been well over an hour. I took one of the last two sips of water out of my bottle and glanced at the map, but there was no information there that tied to anything around me. I set off, faster now, wanting to get to water before I ran out and got too dehydrated. I had passed the little marker that indicated the spring miles ago, not wanting to hump down the slope to get it since I thought I had plenty. I kept going and going, wondering if I had gotten on the wrong trail, but I could see the white blazes. It was definitely the AT. I simply couldn't reconcile the knowledge of my feet and watch with the fact that I hadn't come to the town yet. Had it been swallowed into the earth? Perhaps the ground gave way and even the roads that went through it disappeared. I had been hiking now for about six hours. It was after 2:00 p.m., and I was hungrier than on a normal starved day since I was anticipating a burger for lunch. I was also becoming dehydrated, rationing out the one sip of water remaining in my bottles. Suddenly I saw something that twisted my world upside down and yanked my spirit out through empty gut. It was the shelter I had left that morning.

The day swirled through my head in high speed, rolling over the miles, the time, looking for where I could have turned around and then I realized, it was my one sit-down break to eat. I had indeed been only a few miles from town, but I had been so much in my own head that I stood up and went the wrong way. I was so mad I turned around without even entering the shelter ground and sped down the trail, going as fast as I could. I didn't even think about how hungry or thirsty I was, or that I just walked away from the only good water source without filling up my bottles. An hour later I had slowed, hungry, needing water, bled of frustration over a short day turned into a twenty-four miler. I realized I would need to find that spring again and hope it wasn't dry, or dehydration was going to make for a far more miserable day. The first signs were already beginning with a dull headache and cottonmouth.

I came to the small marker again and dropped off of the trail down a barely used and overgrown path towards a bushy patch that I could tell on approach was a small, shallow spring. It was dribbling out lightly into a tiny puddle, too shallow and muddy for my filter to draw from. Normally I would pass it up for something better, but this was all the water in my world at the moment. I began moving rocks and digging to form a smaller, deeper hole, and then gently swept out as much sediment as I could, waiting patiently for a patch of clean water to gather. Then I gently filled up a bottle so as not to kick up the mud. I drank one on the spot and slowly filled another for the remaining miles which should only take a couple of hours assuming I kept hiking in the right direction.

Now on weary legs I lumbered hungrily along into the afternoon. I was tuned out again, seeing the terrain for the third time that day, when I saw a big puppy rolling around in the grass near the trail playing. I was immediately swept up in his joyful play and dropped my pack so that I could get down on the ground and roll around with him. He didn't care at all about my stupid twenty-four mile day, or how hungry I was, or what could or should happen today. He was just playing because he was alive, chasing the backs of his own eyelids, and was not, it turned out, a dog at all. I was almost to him when I realized it was a bear cub. I froze a few feet away from him and then spun around, looking for his mother. A black bear is a pretty docile animal in most situations, but getting too close to their cubs is a certain way to meet every inch of a momma bear. I slid back to my pack like a ninja, fast, low, and smooth. I flipped it on my back in one motion, and cut a wide path around the cub, who was now looking at me expectantly. I jogged the next mile, and then realized that I was on a long down hill, and spread out before me was Port Clinton.

I had looked at the town map enough to know my way to the Port Clinton Hotel, and I went straight there, had the Hamburger Hiker lunch for dinner, drank some of the local Yuengling beer, and let the sitting become me. I went to the hikers' pavilion near the edge of the small town by the river and set up my gear. It felt very exposed, closer to the road and buildings than the woods, but it would have to do.

I slept there alone, ate from the hotel for breakfast, cleaned my gear, returned to the hotel for lunch, and then sat to read and hope my friends would arrive soon. I poured some more water from one of the many milk cartons full of tap water that locals had provided since there was no water nearby except a river. A river flowing through a town is about the worst place to drink from, second only to standing pond water. It was drizzling lightly and I toyed with my new, ultra-light rain jacket, which would collapse to the size of a fist. I had mailed my heavier Gortex jacket, rain pants, and heavy fleece home a couple weeks earlier, exchanged for lighter summer gear in my mail drop. I had only been cold once in the past weeks. It had rained so hard for so long that day. I had thought it a godsend at first, taking off my shirt and letting the rain cool off my skin and run down my legs, but it kept raining and raining and I had turned very cold. I crouched under a tree for a while hoping for the rain to stop, but it wouldn't, and my body cooled from standing still. Hypothermia was a very real danger, even in the summer, and when I started feeling my mind falter I jolted myself to start hiking again, looking for shelter and getting my body moving. Finally near a road I found an abandoned building full of broken glass and trash and spray-painted graffiti, but out of the rain. I fired up my stove, cooked a hot lunch, and let myself warm and dry by the stove.

The Vikings had had more than enough time now. During the last few days I had expected to see them coming up from behind and hear their whistle through the trees every time I stopped for water or a snack. Now after my backtracking day yesterday and a day of sitting and waiting, I was beginning to wonder if they had gotten off the trail for good. It just didn't make sense. Jones had been in a foul mood the last time I saw him, but quit the trail? And Squirrel. There was no reason in the world for him not to come back as soon as his sister said, "I do." So as night set in again I resolved to spend one more day writing letters and reading, and then I would have to get back up to speed. If I knew for certain they were on the trail behind me, I could keep crawling, but there was no way to be sure, and creeping along at this pace I wouldn't be able to finish the trail this year.

I wrote letters all morning and then headed down the long street that wound its way to the post office, and saw two hikers walking toward me under the overcast sky. They were both shorter than me, one skinny and one stocky, but what I saw most clearly was the stockier one's bouncing swagger that screamed out "Jones!" As I ran to meet them, I recognized that the other hiker was Jokers, but Squirrel was nowhere to be found. The two Vikings hadn't seen any sign of Squirrel since they hiked out of Harper's Ferry. Jones had been off for a week and Jokers had arrived in Harpers Ferry just in time to join him as he got back on. If Squirrel was only a couple of days behind them, then he wasn't trying very hard to catch up. We figured he must have been delayed and would catch us anytime. Jones and Jokers had been keeping a medium pace to catch up to me but not get too far ahead of Squirrel.

We all took another day in the pavilion at Port Clinton, eating well and trying to yogi a ride into a nearby town that had a movie theater. We weren't able to get all the way there, but we managed to get rides to various local landmarks and by a grocery store where we picked up some Ben & Jerry's. Jones had brought new friends with him from the trail behind. Among them was Sir Renity, whom I hadn't seen since the first days on the trail. The bandy-legged veteran stared at me, wondering who this stranger was who shouted his name before recognizing me with hair on my head and face, my body lean and starved. Sir Renity had never known that the Viking Lord, who was always a week ahead of him, was the quiet lad with the shaved head he'd met that first day. Stepping Wolf and Blista were hiking with Sir

Renity. These two friends from Massachusetts hiked near each other though often not together. They wore their athletic builds like warriors but had that trail-worn wisdom in their eyes that spoke of laughter and adventure. They would make excellent Vikings. They brought news from far behind of friends who had left the trail through injury or weariness and told many adventures of their own.

Squirrel had still not come by morning and we finally left the Port Clinton camp, writing in the register to Squirrelfight that we would move slowly to Delaware Water Gap which marked the end of Pennsylvania. We planned to be there for the Fourth of July, but then we were going to have to pick up the pace again, hopefully with Squirrel at our side. When we left Port Clinton, the trail began to turn into the rolling rocks Pennsylvania is famous for on the trail. The fist-sized rocks offered no sure footing, rolling under boots and hiking sticks. Everywhere the ground had eroded into these fist-rocks as if suffering from some kind of mountain disease. The hiking was tough and slow, and the days were long during the second half of Pennsylvania.

I hadn't sent my mail drop to Delaware Water Gap, but to a town one day south of the Gap. When the trail came to the road I broke off from the Vikings, promising to meet them in the Gap before the Fourth. I did my laundry and treated myself to the rare luxury of a motel that sat astride the trail on a highway that stretched into town and beyond, away from the mountains. After all of my waiting for the Vikings, I was strangely glad to be alone. The Viking Camp had been riddled with small stresses in the past days. Jones had seemed generally upset much of the time. The rocks were an obvious pain, but his frustration focused on Jokers, and he would sometimes split off with Stepping Wolf, going ahead to meet with Blista or to be alone. I had really only hiked for a couple of weeks with Jokers all told, and I could see the reasons for Jones' frustration. They didn't dig at me the way they did Jones, but I was ready for another break from Jokers nonetheless. The older hiker's small insecurities about performance and status were out of place twelve hundred miles down the trail, and he was beginning to cling to me since Jones was so obviously upset with him. The Vikings were a flexible group, adding people freely and tolerating all manner of troubles, but Squirrel was part of the core of that ability. I knew how we all supported each other in so many ways, but I hadn't realized how much the Vikings needed Squirrel.

I shook off the discomfort that had settled into a gap in the back of my neck as I was thinking about the tension in camp. I filled my water bottle from the faucet and took a sip, grimacing. The water in towns always tasted like a warm, sour imitation of the mountain spring water I had become accustomed to, but water it was. I sat outside and cooked my supper alone on the concrete walkway in front of the motel as the sun sank deep red into the valley over the town. The soft bed and air conditioning would feel good that night.

In the morning I felt restless. I had woken up later than I wanted to. The sun hadn't come in past the curtains, and the room was dark as night but for a few stale streaks of light at the corners of the curtains. I would reach Delaware Water Gap today, and Squirrel should be aiming for it today also. Could he have passed this little motel already this morning without knowing I was here? I should have left Squirrel a note on the trail by the road. Thoughtless. I pulled on my pack from where it had leaned on the wall all night. It was still packed since I hadn't had to make camp, and I hefted the new food weight from my mail drop. The full pack was down to just over fifty pounds without my winter gear. When I started, it had been over sixty. They say not to carry more than one-third of your body weight, but that allowed seventy pounds for me.

I dropped off my key and walked down the road to the trail and up into the woods. I stepped solidly from rock to rock, hounded by the feeling that Squirrel had already passed me. The rocks of Pennsylvania were trying at times, grueling at others, but now I waded among the endless, fist-sized rocks with little effort, setting a four-mile-an-hour pace. Down the trail about a mile I ran into a couple of hikers coming the other way. They were clean and smelled like shampoo. Day-hikers for sure. I quickly grilled them for information about any other hikers they had passed that morning.

"Sure. There was a pair of them we passed about an hour ago," said the stocky man in front. His dark hair was very neatly combed.

"Did you catch their names?" I probed, hoping for evidence of my friend's passing.

"No, they just humped past us."

"Did one of them have crazy hair like a mop?" I asked, knowing that everyone who met Squirrelfight remembered his hair if not his name.

"Sure," said the day-hiker, smiling.

I moved on possessed. I glided over the rocks and along the bumpy trail. On second thought, crazy hair could mean almost anyone on the trail, but I could feel my friend nearby, and I strode over the rocks as fast as my body could navigate the rolling, sharp boulders. I had been half walking, half jogging for two hours when I came to the first shelter. If Squirrel had passed he would surely have signed in at the shelter. I wound my way up the short path from the trail to where the shelter sat above a dry clearing beaten down in most places to bare dirt. In the shelter a gaggle of what could only be college kids sat snickering and playing with a stove, dressed like they were headed to a frat party. From the edge of the woods came a hiker with the swagger of a newly emptied bladder, but it was a more familiar swagger than that. The hiker wore unfamiliar purple jean cut-offs and a white tank top, browning with layers of sweat, but the heavy boots, dreaded hair, and clear eyes could be none other than the Viking Hero.

"Squirrelfight-snakebite-bobcat-wrestlin-VikingHero!"
I yelled from under my uncontrollable grin, foregoing the
traditional whistle. "How you doin'?"

Squirrelfight looked up in shocked recognition. The
last thing he had expected after his weeks of trying to
catch up to the Vikings was to have the Viking Lord
come up behind him. Squirrelfight took a second lunch
while I rested and we told each other of our time apart. I
could tell Squirrel had been off the trail for a while.
There was something from off of the trail that lingered
around him like a secret. Seeing him in different clothes
continued to be distracting also. We had seen each other
in the same hiking shirt and the same pair of shorts for
months. He told me about his week off that turned into
two, and how he had been hiking twenty- to thirty-mile
days every day through the Pennsylvania rocks to catch
up. He told about reading my and Jones' entries in
registers, rejoicing at every day we took off, and cringing
whenever we wondered if he was gone for good. He told
me about the fifteen-year-old hiker Leap Frog, who had
motivated him to keep up the hard drive to catch up. We
hiked and talked that day, only having to go another six
miles to the Water Gap, and by the time we reached the
summit of the ridge, looking down where the stone layers
of the earth had been shattered making way for the
small town and road, the Viking Hero was back, and
whatever clung to him from off the trail was gone.

We made our way down into town, hoping to catch
Jones unaware and surprise him. We headed first to the
hiker hostel, nestled behind the church, and on the way
ran into Leap Frog waiting on a bench for Squirrel. Leap
Frog was quiet, almost closed off, but became less so on
being introduced to another thru-hiker. He seemed to
have a mild disdain for non-hikers. He had seen Jones
go to the diner down the street with some other hikers
earlier, and expected him back any time. Squirrel and I
took to the street to hunt Jones down. Upon reaching
the road we saw a group of hikers coming back up the
hill from the direction of the diner. Jones and Jokers

were among them and we quickly ducked off the street into the cover of trees between houses.

"Did he see us?" Squirrel grinned, excitement playing across his face.

"I don't know. Let's circle around behind the houses and get behind them," I said, ready for a good hunt. We leaped over a low fence and ran behind the house into the yard. We ran from backyard to backyard leaping over rails and shrubs until I stopped at the back corner of an old house, looking toward the street where the unsuspecting group of hikers limped by, talking among themselves. We jogged quietly to the sidewalk after they passed and then charged up behind them, pouncing on Jones. The Viking Destroyer twirled around, a bewildered look on his face, and we were together again.

We stayed the Fourth, eating ice cream and getting a ride into town to see a movie. Jones was eager to get going, but Squirrel was exhausted after so many days of thirty-milers and convinced him to stay another day to wait for Thursday night, when the church maintaining the hostel brought dishes for a potluck feast fit for a mob of ravished thru-hikers. Many others had similar plans, and still more hurried in over the two days to reach the Water Gap in time for the feast. By Thursday night the tiny parking lot by the church was covered with a long table surrounded by dozens of hikers. We feasted and laughed and met new faces that had come from behind. The horde was reunited, rested, fed, and ready to roam the countryside once more.

CHAPTER 9

A field next to Dennytown Road, New York
1,392 miles down and 776 miles to go

Niday Shelter:
Finally the darkened veil of self-induced monotony has lifted to see again the transparent rays from above in the golden green rainbow which shines forth from the ground below. Glad to be alive and in the woods.

Doubletime
GA > ME

Mailbox Register at Yellow Springs Village site:
Dear Mom, Please send me some dry socks, my youthful optimism, and the blow-up doll in my closet. Thanks Much.

Love,
The Supply Guy
GA > ME

Jones was impatient that morning and left long before we were ready. We had only barely talked him into staying for the Thursday night feast the evening before. There seemed to be something gnawing at his insides, a drive to be finished that was different than our logistic pull towards Katahdin. Squirrel and I were dallying even more than usual because of the rain when a little trail magic breezed in. A local offered to drive our packs to the YMCA camp where we were planning on making our camp that night anyway. Called 'slacking,' this meant he would drive our packs and let us walk unencumbered, and we were certainly willing, only sorry that Jones had already gone and would miss it. Several hikers we had met during the days waiting for the feast also joined in the slack, including a rather sizable group of college kids that had jumped on the trail in Harper's Ferry and was speckled pleasantly with unattached females. A thru-hiker couple, Flower Power and Uncle Wolf were setting their sights on the camp as well and put their packs in the van.

Hiking from Pennsylvania into New Jersey was like slipping into paradise. After weeks of hiking through the hottest, driest, most barren landscape on the trail so far, we passed over the bridge out of the Delaware Water Gap on that rainy morning feeling the moist air flowing through rich green trees. Rain and clouds let everything breathe again. Leaves shed their dry, rough coat and hung heavy and rich. The pale brown path ran dark with lush mud, and by the afternoon the light rain was gone. We walked and talked with the new hikers, watching birds and resting on rock outcroppings and vistas that had been rare in Pennsylvania. Late in the day we caught Jones setting up camp by himself on an overlook short of our planned camp, frustrated that we hadn't caught up all day, and we urged him to pack up his gear and continue on with us. Two counselors met us at the YMCA camp and showed us a large cabin with beds and a kitchen and bathroom. The counselors said we could stay as long as we liked. There was a lake and other cabins nearby, and across the lake were hordes of screaming children just out of earshot. The section that became the Viking Camp was the old summer camp, now abandoned by the kids but kept up by the staff. We stayed that night and through the next day when the sun beat down clean and hot. We found the facilities much to our liking and spent much of the day at the lake on raft-like islands that framed the camper's old swimming area. The cold water soothed our tired muscles and bones, washing away the heat and hurt. Even after we had taken several days off in the Gap, none could argue the perfection of taking this second break a day later, and Squirrel needed all the rest he could get.

This new and larger horde made of both thru-hikers and section-hikers from Harper's Ferry stayed together for a while after the YMCA. Grover, Whichway, and Raven were still with us the night we made camp on top of the look-out tower at High Point, New Jersey. That night, a great storm ripped over us as a reminder of how foolish and vulnerable we were, tented out on the exposed platform. By morning not a piece of gear was dry, no matter how well protected, and few of us had slept, fearing that one of the lightning bolts crashing down all around us would grab hold of the metal poles in our tent, shearing life and limb. In the days following High Point, though, rain scarcely came, and everywhere we went were stories of drought. Springs dried up and ponds were sunk to murky puddles. The temperature rose until the sun was so cruel that it was foolish to hike under it. We would spend the hottest part of the day at lakes fighting off bugs or inside, if a building presented itself. We would hike in the late afternoon and into evening and night, waking up before the sun to hike a bit before finding a place to hide through the middle of the day. Since many springs had run dry, locals would often post signs at road crossings offering their houses for water and shade. Once, a local supermarket even hauled gallons of water to a place along the trail where water was scarce.

The heat demanded our attention and obedience. It reached 104 degrees in the shade one day and we heard at a shelter that a day-hiker had died from heat stroke. Even attempts to move short distances in the middle of the day were futile drudgery. The heat sucked energy and motivation at every step. At night I would lie in my tent without my sleeping bag. I couldn't even touch it. I needed my tent to survive the bugs, but I would set it up without the rain fly so it couldn't trap any heat. Luckily my tent was all netting above the six-inch mud break, so when there was wind I could get the most out of it. I would lie on my sleeping pad through the hot night wearing only my bike shorts, praying for a breeze that brought something other than heat.

One evening the Viking horde camped along-side a tiny dirt road. Camping close to a road of any kind was generally to be avoided, but this one seemed to be pretty remote. More importantly, it was home to a small shed with a water pump nailed into the ground like a needle into a vein of the earth, and we happily pumped quart after quart. The gravel road broke out of the trees and cut across a wide field where the shed and pump were stationed. We set up tent city in the field so we could have as much water as we wanted for dinner, cleaning, breakfast, and hiking the next day. The tents were scattered over the field in multicolored patches, and we cleared a wide spot near the shed under a tree to feast. All the stoves lit up in a tattered ring in the growing darkness, and the smell of fuel and the hiss of the flames were gradually replaced by the smell of dinner and the sound of jostling dishes. Jones, Squirrel, and myself were masters at the art of the feast. We pot-lucked every night and invited anyone camped with us to join in. We used dehydrated vegetables, dried meats, spices and heavy doses of butter from squeeze bottles to make our potlucks memorable. Many a hard day gave in to dreaming about dinner, and we never let each other down. New Vikings couldn't always be trusted to offer up the best of dishes, but some blandness would be tolerated for a while in the interest of fellowship.

Around the circle were the faces of new friends lit by the soft glow of the darkening sky and the flickering of stove flames under pots. We hadn't known any of these people more than a week or so, but in such close quarters we were quickly coming to know each other well. Such was the way of the trail. Saprophite and Eft were an odd couple hunched over their large pot of Ramen noodles with meat-textured vegetable protein mixed in. They were part of the group out of Harper's

Ferry that had split off before Delaware Water Gap and had since joined the rest of their group and the Vikings. Their relationship, which was spiraling into ruin, was a point of stress in their group. Their meat-textured vegetable protein was a point of stress for the Vikings. It tasted like it looked, chewy and off-white. It seemed like the moment they finally broke up, Eft would leave the trail. He seemed to be there only for Saprophite, while she was in the woods to hike. Whatever was going to happen, it could only happen fast in such close quarters. Raven was Sapro's roommate from college. She was a tall, dark-haired birdwatcher sitting cross-legged behind her steaming pot of mac n' cheese, a standard but acceptable dish with enough butter. Over the last week she and I had attempted and ended a short relationship, though it still lingered about the camp.

Grover kneeled over his Lipton noodles and pointed his headlamp in the pot to see if the excess water had boiled off. He was quick to laugh and fell into stride with the Viking ways easily. He had been with Whichway since we met them in Delaware Water Gap, but she had since fallen behind. WhichWay had only a short while, perhaps two months, to be on the trail and was entertaining thoughts of ending her hike even earlier. Except for meeting Grover, she had had nothing but ill fortune. She had suffered through a concussion, a dog bite, terrible sunburn at the YMCA, and finally Lyme disease. Her enthusiasm over her "vacation" was understandably waning. A few days earlier she had stayed behind in Unionville, New York, where we had stopped to pick up supplies and have some fruit in the shade and ice cream if we could find any. Grover left Unionville with the Vikings at her request. WhichWay was waiting on some supplies that hadn't arrived and she chose to keep waiting, promising to catch up if she could. She didn't want Grover to get behind everyone else on her account. We were pretty sure we wouldn't see her again. There was something about the way people held themselves when they were ready to leave the trail.

Some slight satisfaction and some remorse, but mostly it was their refusal of help and support that signaled the end. There was always a way to keep hiking if the will was there, but once that will broke, a powerful certainty fell in its place.

Cooking something that smelled remarkably like pesto was the new newspaper writer from the same newspaper relay team as Tall Grass Prairie. He and the new photographer who called himself Flash Shurpa had caught us a few days earlier, and Flash had been hiking with the Vikings a bit. He was as excited about his assignment as we were about their dinner, but the writer didn't seem quite as enthusiastic. Apparently, the whole reporter-relay-hike had been his idea, but he had unknowingly picked the toughest time to be on the trail for himself with the heat and the drought. Flash was in heaven, though, and for an outdoorsman he had been dealt a pretty good hand. The reporters had all their gear and food paid for and got their regular salary while they were in the woods hiking. It sounded too good to be true. The writer was older and quieter and needed to be given a trail name. He sat poking at his creation, opening little jars and measuring tiny morsels of flavor over the edge and into his pot. Jones was finished and ready to eat, tasting his food but waiting for everyone else to be ready. He leaned over the writer's pot and dipped his spoon into the steaming darkness to sample the flavor.

"Oh, Papa," he said with an Italian accent, "Papa Gino. Is'a somthin'a'special tonight!"

"Whatcha got there, Papa Gino?" I said, peeking over across the circle. My spinach and parmesan noodles with bits of chicken had been done for a few minutes and the lid was on.

"It's his special homemade pesto," said Flash eagerly. Papa Gino was still quiet. "He's quite a gourmet."

The piping hot dishes were all shoved to the middle of the circle where they collected into a wide platform of steaming goodness. Sitting or on our knees, we began to sample from all the pots, tasting, sighing, and finally filling our overturned pot lids with heavy portions. Quiet descended but for the rattle of spoons on lids and the slopping of food in mouths. We ate and ate until our bellies were stuffed, and the group fell into sporadic chatter as the dishes with food remaining were very slowly emptied by hesitant spoons. As we finished up in the deepening dark, holding heavy bellies and making trips to the pump to clean dishes and fetch water, the horde began readying itself to retire to the tents.

Suddenly there was a faint noise that stopped everyone's chatter and perked every ear in camp. We were like a herd of hunted elk. The growing shift and pop of gravel and dirt was unmistakable. A car was coming. The growl of an engine and the patter of tire-tossed debris came menacingly closer. Locals at night didn't necessarily mean trouble, but a hiker's worst nightmare started like this. We all sat still in the dark hoping the car would go on by us. We would be easy to miss if one wasn't looking. The tents were somewhat hidden by the shed, and we were huddled under a tree in the dark.

A white van burst from behind the shed along the road and growled past, its angles and smells strange and foreboding. The sides of the van were covered with paintings impossible to make out between the night and the headlights. The van started to slow and finally turned to a stop only a stone's throw down the road. Bright headlights angled back around and whipped toward us, blazing over our dinner gathering. We were spotted. We all sat motionless, listening, watching, waiting to hear the unbalanced babble of a psychopath or the terrifying twang of local misfits. The silence held us and stretched thinner and thinner. We were all silently making decisions about whether to charge in an attack or flee to the woods without our gear. Jones suddenly broke the tableaux, leaning forward and squinting into the light with a look of a shifting puzzlement.

"Is that...an ice cream truck?" As we peered at the bright lights, apprehension gave way to confusion. I hefted myself onto stiff legs and went to investigate the van stopped some twenty yards from our camp. Approaching the vehicle I could see that the Viking Destroyer was correct! This didn't necessarily rule out the possibility of sudden violence, but it did open up an entirely new set of possibilities. It was my office as the Viking Lord to deal with foreign diplomats, and several other Vikings fell in behind me. I circled around the window as a chubby, tired-looking man leaned over.

"Do you know what time it is?" said the ice cream man.

"It's about thirty minutes after sunset. Do you have *ice cream*?" I was still dealing with some caution, for this was obviously no ordinary encounter and the presence of angels or demons was likely.

"Yeah, um, I guess. Hold on." The ice cream man reached back behind him and pulled open the window and deck that folded off the side of the truck. As the counter leaned out, the light inside came on, revealing the colorful menu board and ice cream paintings on the side of the truck. As the man appeared in the window of the ice cream truck, canned nursery rhymes began to dance across the field. Everyone flocked to the bizarre oasis. The light from the window spread over a small semicircle beside the truck, and into the light we came. It was too strange to bother thinking about.

"I'll have an ice cream sandwich," I said, and out came the treasure, frosty steam trailing from it in the night's heat. And so we went, lining up and placing our orders with patient excitement, money in hand, and one by one walked away with ice cream. All but Squirrel.

"No way," said the Viking. "This is too strange. I won't participate in a mass hallucination." Perhaps he was right. Biting into my ice cream sandwich, I took in the scene with suspicion. Saprophite was on her tiptoes, elbows on the counter awaiting her Pushup Pop. The cool white light illuminated her hair and wide eyes, several bugs spiraling in the halo, and dropped off where the rest of the line willed itself forward in fear that the

114

hallucination would end before they had a chance to partake. The truck disappeared back the way it came, and aside from the ice cream wrappers in our trash bags there was nothing about the little touch of relief from the heat that we could connect with reality. Squirrel persisted in the assertion that we all were hallucinating under the influence of meat-textured vegetable protein poisoning.

CHAPTER 10

Mount Greylock, Massachusetts
1,559 miles down and 609 miles to go

Limestone Springs Lean-to:
A not particularly restful night at all. Supply Guy and I spent the night thrashing around in our respective sleeping bags, trying to find positions in which we could be safe from the squadrons of ravenous mosquitoes and also be able to breathe. I know I failed, and by the difficulty Supply Guy is having filtering a quart of water, I don't think he got much sleep either. Fortunately we still have our sanity. I think. Ho ho ho hee hee hee ha ha.

The Ordainer
GA > Purgatory

I could see Jones and Squirrel up ahead near the edge of the field. Jones was slapping Squirrel around the back of the head as he had been doing for most of the day. The deer flies loved Squirrel's matted, thick hair, and would gather in it to crawl and bite. Jones had also been targeted by a steady onslaught of bugs. I told him it was because they knew he was taking it personally. I hadn't minded the deer flies so much. Perhaps I had less trouble since I hiked in back and the flies had their fill of blood by the time I rolled along. The main reason they didn't get to me, though, was that their bite, while painful, was over when they were gone. What drove me crazy were the mosquitoes. The trail had been dipping by swamps and bogs through Connecticut and Massachusetts, and the evil little armies would rise off the marshy floor in clouds. We would start hiking faster, hoping to outrun all but the most diligent, but looking down I would see six or ten little insect blood wells set up on each arm and a kind of skittish insanity would set in. A moment later, when my arms were coated with second-hand blood and little hair-like legs and wings, the itching would start, and the only way to survive was not to scratch. Bees were also in the habit of building their nests in the earth of the trail so that when one of us walked over the underground nest they would swarm and sting. It seemed all our exposed skin was covered in welts from one bug or another.

Camp became a hurried affair. The luxury of taking off hot stinky boots to air out tired, battered feet was an invitation to bites all over the ankles, feet and toes. For some reason—perhaps it was the smell—mosquitoes regarded feet as a delicacy; more likely, the devils knew how sensitive our feet were and that the bites would itch unbearably. The foot was right up there with the knuckle on the list of the worst places to be bitten.

Dinners were cooked, water filtered, and tents set up and sealed faster than ever. For the first time, our constant relaxed pace was beginning to elude us. The small towns of New England were quaint and pristine, clean and expensive. The wonderful little roadside fruit stands we had patronized in New York and New Jersey were replaced by the pricey deli or cafe. The only prices that stayed the same were three-dollar pints of Ben & Jerry's and free water, and as luck would have it, that was all we needed to survive. Whenever we left towns we were soon back in the swamp.

The Harper's Ferry crew caught up or passed us occasionally, but we rarely camped together any more and even more seldom hiked together. We had left the larger group one evening when the multitude of criss-crossing relationships was having a noticeable effect on the overall mood of the camp. We hadn't hiked all those hundreds of miles to be returned to the disorienting web of influences in which the world off the trail trapped the soul. This group from Harper's Ferry had lost none of their social intertwining since they all knew each other from before their hike. They hadn't experienced the cleansing solitude of beginning the trail alone. They had trail names but were not transformed. As long as they stayed together, they were just as they had been, only in a different place. On the evening of our departure we hiked hard and fast a few more hours in single file to a road and down to a gas station to get water. Cooking dinner on the pavement in front of the dark station we ate together and were one again. Two days later the Harper's Ferry group caught up to us again, but we no longer pot-lucked together.

We were a unified trio, but spirits flagged a little in spite of our solidarity. During the day we trudged through the heat and mosquitoes and deer flies over pastures and through swamps, and though Squirrel's fortified good nature seemed to be pulling him through, Jones' complaints could be heard for miles, and I was quietly and steadily losing my mind. Every time I looked down and saw my flesh covered with mosquitoes, I thought the next time I would snap. The nights were unusually quiet and without laughter. The muffled sound of scratching and uncomfortable shifting sifted between the tents, and mosquitoes stalked the mesh walls looking for holes. We got our break just in time.

Jones had been talking about the Harbor Day festival in his college town for months, and one of his fraternity brothers drove to the trail to pick us up from the Berkshires and take us clear across the State of New York to Oswego, where the mosquitoes had to struggle for survival in the concrete valley. We rested and ate and enjoyed the hospitality of Jones' fraternity brothers and family for almost a week and on my birthday went to a Renaissance festival where I bought colorful leather masks almost like animal faces or wild men for each of us. We found the ninety-nine-cent Whopper and the ninety-nine-cent Seven-Layer Burrito. For the first time in months we could eat in town affordably, because four of either of these bargains would fill us nicely.

We spent time with Jones' fraternity brothers, those still in school and many who had graduated. Squirrel and I were completely out of our element, and despite being in town for so long, I remained Wayah. Jones' brothers wrapped their arms around us despite our differences because we were brothers to Jones and nothing else mattered to them. There was something very familiar about their complete acceptance of us and their willingness to do anything they could for us, and I began to see why Jones might be frustrated by so much of the trail. Among his brothers, family didn't involve discomfort after discomfort. Their adventures lasted an evening, and there were no shortages of showers, soft beds, food, or girls. The last night we were there, Squirrel and I lay waiting for sleep and talking about how their family had many things in common with ours, but how the trail made us feel powerful and driven, and this party that rekindled itself night after night gave us a feeling of stagnation, however comfortable. It had also, however, given us a long rest and let us build back the blood the mosquitoes had stolen.

Then we were back in the woods, but the rest had rejuvenated us, allowing us to gather up our spirits and allowing Jones to bathe in the familiar. The heat was more bearable when we returned, the woods seemed fresher, and Kaptain Krummholz wasn't far behind. We had passed him when he was off the trail, taking a break to go to Israel. Now the gap had narrowed during our break in Oswego, allowing him time to catch up.

The night of our return we caught Screaming Coyote limping along the trail and camped with him at the shelter. Squirrel had passed him before when he was hiking long days through Pennsylvania to catch up, but Jones and I had only heard about him. That night he told us his story. A year earlier he had been wrestling with a friend and hurt his neck a little. A blood clot formed silently, fired off into his brain, and caused a stroke that paralyzed his left side. Doctors said he would probably never walk again, which he took as a challenge. After a year of physical therapy, he started the Appalachian Trail on the anniversary of his stroke. He had trouble moving his left arm and his left leg seemed unwieldy, but he had made it 1,500 miles and it didn't look like he planned on stopping. He handed his water bottle to me and asked if I could open it for him. The question caught me off guard. I looked at Coyote's slightly twisted left hand, wry and smiling face, curly blonde hair dangling around his broad forehead, scraggly beard, and deep-set, bright eyes, and I was truly impressed. Not because Coyote had hiked so far or suffered through so much, but because he continued to love it all. He could have been fighting his way along just to spite his doctors and his body, but he had risen higher. Anger is the least of the powers available to the human spirit and the easiest. Coyote had found a greater strength in joy and good company. He was a Viking long before he met the Horde. None of the problems in my gut could compare to his burdens, and no one could carry them more lightly than he did. Coyote wasn't broken; he just did better with help. So do I. I thought about my stomach and why I was on the trail. I looked hard at Jones and thought about what silent burdens he might have loaded in his pack.

Two days later in Dalton, Massachusetts, in the midst of the overwhelming hospitality of Tom Levardi, who was letting hikers camp in his yard and feeding us tremendously, we saw Flash Shurpa again with a new partner, Brutus; Tadpole and Danger Moose with his hula-hoop; and two brothers from Denmark who were hiking a section. First thing in the morning, the Kaptain came strolling down the street grinning through his huge red beard, which had grown noticeably since Trail Days. He had realized we were just ahead and had come in early from the shelter a few miles back. The sunlight washed kindly over the trail that day.

In my Dalton mail drop, I got a new pair of spandex bike shorts. They were just in time. I wore spandex under my shorts to cut down on chafing, and both pairs I had were worn out and disintegrating at the seams. That night I put on the new ones, ready to feel the material against my skin, but they were too tight and the fabric stretched to roughness. I thought if I just slept in them they would break in, but apparently spandex is stronger than flesh, and after a few hours of hiking the next morning, I realized that I was losing the grinding battle with the shorts, and worse, they were actually chafing me in the most unspeakable of places. I couldn't go on. The Vikings gathered at a small, rocky break in the trees to discuss solutions to my unusual and embarrassing dilemma. I had put my tattered old spandex back on, but it was too late. Every step tormented my new wounds.

"What's in your first aid kit?" asked Jones. "Could you just wrap some tape around it?" Squirrel started laughing in a pained whine. I looked through my first aid kit for relief. I had antibiotic ointment to heal it, but I needed something to protect and cover the wound. Gauze wrapping and medical tape—I had a whole roll of each. I had begun to question the logic of carrying medical supplies with so few uses, but today they were worth the months with the extra weight.

"I'm sorry, but I can't be with you for this," said Squirrel, half smiling. "I'm going to head on. Good luck."

"That's all right. I'd kind of like to be alone right now anyway." I wobbled off into the woods to begin my bandaging. The operation muted the pain passably, and I was up and walking again soon, if carefully.

The morning was hazy and cool as we climbed up Mt. Greylock and rainy as we climbed down the steep slope starting to run with mud. I slid and took a nasty spill, driving my knee into a rock just as the rain began to come down hard. My boots filled with water despite my gaiters, and my raincoat was useless since the air was so warm that I was as wet from sweat in the jacket as I would have been from rain outside. Rain dripped off the brim of my hat into my face and ran down my arms and legs into my boots. Sloshing along, favoring my bashed knee, and constraining my hip movements as much as possible on a steep downhill, I was about to scream out that I was having my worst day on the trail when I thought of my genitals wrapped carefully in gauze and secured with medical tape and I began to laugh. Every jolt of pain or uncomfortable slosh of spongy sock made the comedy greater, and I laughed uncontrollably down the trail, imagining how foolish I must seem, and where Coyote must be now, every moment of his day more challenging than this one.

I couldn't remember when anything had happened that had made me seriously consider leaving the trail, and by the time we reached the halfway point, such thoughts seemed impossible. Even now, with the heat and the mosquitoes and my bad day, nothing was more obvious than the fact that the day would end, likely among friends, food, and laughter. The heat was beginning to wane with the coming of September, and with it would go the mosquitoes. We had only 600 miles and three states left to go, and even though we had two months of the hardest hiking on the trail left, Mount Katahdin was very much within reach. It had always loomed behind our shorter goals, but now it didn't seem so far away considering how far we had already come. Remembering the long map on the wall in Hot Springs, North Carolina, I saw that it was now a trek more behind us than ahead of us. In our minds the Vikings had already begun the assault on Katahdin.

CHAPTER 11

Manchester Center, Vermont
1,622 miles down and 546 miles to go

Zion Episcopal Church Hostel Register:
*"And how will I know these Vikings?" asked the young
boy.*

"They carry no packs," replied the old sage.

"No packs?" he exclaimed wide-eyed.

*"They have others carry their possessions," said the
old gray sage knowingly.*

"I don't understand."

*"They have powers," whispered the sage, "Diabolical
powers." The young boy quivered.*

Anonymous

Limestone Springs Lean-to:
*Wow, I am so grateful for the cool weather today. Stayed
at Silver Hill last night & trying for Riga tonight. If we
make it, this will be my longest day yet. Looking at the
map, it seems doubtful, but the cool weather has given me
a second wind. Hello to Lone Scout.*

Jingo

GA > ME

*P.S. Ludo, who has no interest in writing but only eating
says, "Real life sucks, hike on."*

Crossing into Vermont was like drinking from the
fountain of youth. The weather was finally becoming
what we had long wished for, and our bodies and minds
were fine-tuned to the hike. The breeze blew cool without

being humid and the rich green mountains gave plenty of shade and cold water. Even the air had a sweet, cheery smell to it. Our first Vermont re-supply point was in Manchester Center, a colorful little resort town at the foot of beautiful ski slopes turned verdant and sunny in the off-season. It was five-and-a-half miles off the trail and we planned to hitch in. Jones and I got to the well groomed, two-lane road first and began to walk toward town, thumbs out and watching for a good ride. We had become quite used to hitchhiking in the past months. It was the best way to get into a town that was too far off the trail to walk without losing the better part of a day. We had had some creepy rides from local crazies and some really friendly ones that might offer fruit or sodas or even a shower. Usually we just flung ourselves in the back of someone's truck and thanked them when we hopped out. It was probably the most vulnerable aspect of life on the trail, but an essential part of hiker life, and statistically not as dangerous as driving to work in the morning.

Jones and I stood a good chance of getting a ride. The pack was a big help in trail towns where the locals knew that hikers were around and needed rides, but even then, a lone hiker could have trouble getting a ride. Two men together actually stood a much better chance and felt safer as well. Three or more was trouble. Three hikers and packs would fit in no less than an empty truck, and any more than five needed a U-haul. The college kids in the black jeep that picked us up were the perfect ride. They were interested in the trail, and the open jeep kept our smell from gathering too thickly. I had read in the *Thru-hiker's Handbook* that there was a Ben & Jerry's store in Manchester Center and asked about it immediately, offering to buy some ice cream in thanks for the ride. Within minutes we were standing on the posh New England sidewalk looking up at the most glorious of signs. Those bright, colorful letters had been nothing but good to us for so many long months. We had endured the Southern states, where we were lucky to find two or three flavors, and always the same ones. As we had approached the B & J homeland, the selection had grown. When we pushed past the glass door we were faced with a board covered with names and flavors that boggled the mind. Tubs of goodness were lined up in rows under glass shields just thick enough to prevent any hasty advances.

"The Vermonster," Jones said, standing to the side of the counter reading an advertisement that I had been too mesmerized to notice. "Twenty scoops of Ben & Jerry's, five cups of hot fudge, five cups of nuts, two large brownies, five cups of crushed cookies." The words started to come slower as Jones' voice trailed into a high-pitched mixture of excitement and amazement. "Whipped cream, bananas, strawberries, sprinkles." Jones took a picture of the sign.

"We'd like the Vermonster please." I was all business now. The girl behind the counter slid over a piece of paper and a pencil for us to write down the flavors we wanted. "All right. Everybody now." I motioned to the college kids, who hovered uncertainly nearby. "C'mon. This is your reward for being kind to stinky strangers." I was grinning, but had some urgency in my voice. This was no time for hesitation. We made the list and I checked it over for flavor balance and melting order stability, and soon there was a huge salad-tossing bowl in the middle of our table spilling over with whipped cream and fruit. It was quite a dig before we got to the ice cream. The battle was long and well fought, and in victory we passed the bowl around, taking sips of the mixed flavor soup that was left in the bottom, speckled with sprinkles and wisps of hot fudge.

Jones and I hiked with painfully full bellies over to the hostel where we found that Squirrel and Krummholz had arrived and were in the midst of preparing a burrito feast. I was only able to eat one burrito and they looked on in horror, which changed to amazement and grief as Jones and I described our battle with the Vermonster. We agreed that in the morning we would return and battle a second ice cream beast as a horde. Again it was a glorious effort and the Vikings emerged victorious. As a symbol of the good fight, I sewed a Ben & Jerry's patch to my pack over a hole where a mouse had chewed in an attempt to get the juggling balls Brooke had made for me, which apparently had some rice in them.

Squirrel's parents, who lived in New Hampshire, were vacationing at a drive-in campground in Vermont as we were passing through. They came to pick us all up several days in a row, bringing us to their camper each night to feed us big dinners and breakfasts under a wide awning before taking us back to the trail to slack the next day. When they came to the trail they would bring beer and snacks and hamburgers for us and any other hikers who happened along. Back at the campground where their trailer sat nestled in a small lot, thinly divided from other camping lots by trees, Mama Squirrelfight fed us enormous helpings of sausage, potatoes, steak, and corn, and would not stop until we were immobile. We only had meat in small quantities over the last five months and all the Viking's bowels were shot from the sudden overdose. The second night Kaptain Krummholz joined us at the campsite and stayed during the following days of slacking and feasting.

It was good to have the Kaptain around for many reasons. First, he was a good Viking, and his company was always a pleasure. Second, he rejuvenated some of the flagging spirits that had been bringing the Vikings down in the past weeks. Squirrel and I had been worried about Jones, whose mood rarely seemed to improve. Any day that wasn't the best day of his life was the worst, and the fact that Squirrel and I weren't suffering similarly only drove him away from us and deeper into his funk. The arrival of the Kaptain, though, brought him back up a bit. Aside from being a source of humor and creativity, the Kaptain had different experiences and trail stories from ours. The new dynamic had added a new flavor to our hike. The Kaptain was also an excellent trail cook who appreciated the Vikings' grand feasts and always had something worthy to add. In fact, he became the most insistent that newer Vikings bring worthy food to the potluck. The Kaptain always wore a graying hat that had a big "V" on the forehead.

"The girl who gave it to me said that I had to say it stood for vaginal canal," the Kaptain said, laughing.

"You know, of course, that it really stands for Vikings, don't you?" I said, only half joking. Krummholz just chuckled and shook his head.

Slack-packing is a subject of some debate on the trail. Stemming from a hiker's notion of purism, some felt that not carrying a pack was cheating. To me, the adventure surrounding the slack—the faster, unencumbered hiking over longer distances—was as much a part of the adventure as anything else. Squirrelfight felt that as long as he was hiking every part of the trail, it didn't matter if he carried five pounds or 65 or went naked. Jones was always glad for the break, and Krummholz was too busy having a good time to worry about what anyone thought about how he was hiking. In all, there was no objection among the Vikings to taking advantage of a slack as often as one came up, and in Vermont they came up a lot. After slacking much of the first half of Vermont with the aid of Squirrel's parents, Squirrelfight's brother came out and slacked us southward through the last half of Vermont. We would leave our packs in his car and he would drop off half of the group at one end of the day's hike and drive to the other end to leave the car and hike the other way with the other half of the group. The two groups would meet for lunch in the middle, and then continue on. The group that reached the car would then go and pick up the other. Then we would camp near the road with all our gear ready and available. Going backwards provided a new treat. First, we were skipping three days ahead to start, so we would run into anyone that was up to three days ahead of us, many of whom we would not see again on the trail, since we were taking more time off when we came near Squirrel's house in New Hampshire. Second, by the time we finished slacking backwards for three days, we were three days behind the actual distance we had hiked on the trail and could see people who were up to three days behind us.

We zigzagged over Vermont's last 45 miles with Squirrel's brother in tow, playing like kids in someone else's back yard. When we came to a bridge, we would jump off it. When we passed a place with a funny name (like Podunk), we would make up a song about it. By the time Jones and I reached Happy Hill Cabin heading south, Squirrel, Krummholz and Jason (Squirrel's brother) had just arrived heading north. Happy Hill Cabin was the picture of neglect. It seemed instead of maintaining the shelter, it had been used for caging rhinoceroses from time to time. More likely it was being used for college parties and had lost its potential to be useful for anything else. The porch, though, still offered shade and rails to lean on. Jason was flipping through the register and looking at entries, while Krummholz and Squirrel pulled out their lunches and waited their turn. We all sat and talked about those we had passed, and we traded the car keys and information about what the other group would see when they walked the next half of the day.

"Some of these people seem to be really mad at everyone else on the trail." Jason said, half amused and half concerned. I leaned over to see the entries and their authors.

"Oh, yeah. Those guys are always going on and on, but they're more self-righteous than mad. There's a few like that up ahead."

"Probably behind, too," Squirrel said. "We just don't get to read their entries." Jones looked up from the paper he had been reading.

"Damn purists. They should just hike their own hike and leave everyone else out of it." By the time he had finished his sentence, Jones was looking back at the paper again. It was true that in the last month, the register discussions on pure thru-hiking had taken on an even darker, more exclusive tone than those in the south. In trail discussions, purism had come to refer to the notion that unless very strict rules were followed in hiking the trail, a hiker should be shunned from the thru-hiking community. The most common gripe was with hikers who had skipped sections of the trail, but particularly whiny hikers held dozens of laws that they claimed disqualified nearly everyone but themselves.

"This guy is saying that anyone who didn't hike the approach trail to the Appalachian Trail isn't really a thru-hiker!" Jason read in disbelief.

"He's just mad because those eight extra miles kicked his ass and then he found out he could have driven right to the trail head," Squirrel said grinning. We all laughed. "It amazes me that someone could hike this whole trail and still be so insecure. You would think hiking 2,000 miles would boost their self-esteem a little."

"I don't know how many times one of those guys has disqualified me from thru-hiker status," Krummholz said. "Either I was carrying too much weight, carrying too little weight, looking at the ground too much, making too many phone calls..."

"No sense of humor," I said as Jason handed the register over to Squirrel and shuddered.

"More politics out here than I would have expected," Jason said. I laughed.

"Yeah," I said, "well, at least we can just turn the page on them."

CHAPTER 12

Galehead Hut, the White Mountains, New Hampshire
1,798 miles down and 370 miles to go

Gentian Pond Shelter:
Met Key-Mho-Saw-Bee (I'm about as happy with that spelling as I was with the AMC hut 'croos') on my way up Mount Hayes this morning. He told me I look nothing like a thru-hiker (I'm not happy with that spelling either) and said that I'm the fattest one he's seen on the trail. I said, 'Gee, thanks' and then I punched him in the mouth. When I combine his observations with the other things I've learned about myself from other hikers over the past couple of days, I discover that I am a slow, fat, scary-looking guy with a nice butt who has aroused a lot of suspicion that I may not be a purist. Golly, this journey of self-discovery is a joyous thing.

The Ordainer (previously called Buzzsaw)
GA > teen crisis hotline

Our first order of business upon entering New Hampshire was to go to the Squirrelfight household and take a week off. After almost a week off in Massachusetts and then slacking most of Vermont we didn't need a break, but Squirrel had to be in a friend's wedding, and we weren't about to let him get a week behind so close to the end. The Kaptain went on ahead only because he was going to take a break in the next few days for a week also, and we would be able to meet up in the White Mountains. The days at Squirrel's house were quiet and domestic: eating homemade cookies, watching TV and movies, and throwing a baseball in the yard. We all longed for the trail, though, and were back on as soon as the wedding was over.

We hiked into New Hampshire for four days before getting off one last time to hitch back to Vermont for the Bread and Puppet festival. It wasn't easy, taking another break so quickly when the last wasn't even necessary. So close to Katahdin, the pull of our long-awaited goal was immense. Squirrel promised it would be an adventure, though, and we agreed to one last delay. We hitched from a tiny road that wound around the foot of the White Mountains, the first time the trail would break out above tree-line, and held the sight of the rocky peaks with us, waiting to dive into those high mountains when we returned.

The festival consisted of various puppet shows and dramatizations from finger puppets to gargantuan icons that towered over weaving dancers and colorful costumes. Near the shows were colorful shops and stands selling ethnic foods and wild and woven crafts. One of the attractions that gave the festival its name was a stand that baked bread and gave it away for free. There were so many people in line, though, that we opted instead to buy Indian finger foods. In the "Parking Lots," expanses that had once been grassy meadow were covered with cars, tents, fires, and coolers. The multitudes that covered these fields far outnumbered the onlookers at the puppet shows. We discovered that most of this second crowd's purpose consisted of roaming the lots, abusing as many substances as they could find, and making sure that neither they nor anyone else slept. Jerry Garcia had died a few weeks earlier before doing a show in Boston, and a legion of lost Deadheads had found their way to Bread and Puppet in their search for a surrogate source of meaning. The nights were tiring. The inebriated and the reckless threatened constantly to destroy our tents or gear with a bad step or misplaced flaming log. The commotion was a bit much after five months of relative serenity. The days were much more interesting. We wandered the shows, acts, and exhibits, entirely free of the crowd that never left the lots. We saw Fur Trapper for the first time since Harper's Ferry. He caught a ride down to the festival with Buzzsaw, who had changed his name in Pennsylvania to the Ordainer, since a section-hiker ahead of him had been using the name also, and he couldn't seem to catch up to him and straighten him out. We had not seen Buzzsaw since Trail Days, and Fur Trapper since just after leaving Rusty's. Fur Trapper was already in Maine, only a handful of days from finishing the Trail, but Buzzsaw was already finished and back at home in Maine when he had run into Fur Trapper. We also saw Fly for the first time since before Trail Days. She and Aces had finished about the same time as Buzzsaw. It was bizarre seeing Fly and Buzzsaw, knowing they had already finished. In the registers, their comments occupied the present even though the date was much earlier. It always felt as if the writer of an entry had just walked down the path before the reader got there. To read their entries and imagine them off the trail was very hard. They were already starting to incorporate elements of town life into themselves. They had schedules and clean socks, but their heads still floated in the mild euphoria of the trail, and they slipped easily into the potluck and the tent. The last night of the festival we all sat on the sloping hills around the field that served as a stage for the largest shows during the festival but had slipped into darkness. We howled in the night to the silky animal replies of strangers and smiled at the stars.

Buzzsaw drove us back to the trail with Fur Trapper through light rain, and we were back in the woods. There was nothing but the trail now leading from our feet, through the Whites, into Maine, through the Hundred Mile Wilderness, and up the rocky face of Katahdin.

We had begun to pass the occasional south-bounder in Massachusetts. The few who chose to hike south had to start much later, waiting until Baxter State Park, where Katahdin stood monumental, opened for the year.

They would usually saunter up with an elitist slant telling of the great northern mountains that would surely be our fall. It was a tradition of sorts, and we would smile and resist the temptation to say, "Sparky, I've been in the mountains six times as long as you now. I think I'll be just fine." The good ones were those who came by and exchanged knowing smiles with us, both envying what lay ahead of the other. We had come 1,800 miles to take the steps ahead, and each one was a reward.

We had our cold weather gear mailed back to us while we were at Squirrel's house. I had to turn in my boots, which were finally caving in. The soles were separating around the toe, and the constant caking of salt from my sweat had finally broken down the metal studs that held the laces and the leather around them, letting water in. Now I had to wear my spares. They weren't as good—really just sturdy work boots—but they only had to last 450 miles.

Up over the tree line we soared on the back of Mt. Moosilauke and into the Whites. These summits surpassed even my dreams of the trail. The stark slabs of speckled rock ripped through the trees like shouts of primal nature, reigning over the land. The clouds gathered at the mountains' feet and swirled up the sheer faces. We marched across the Presidential range, their rocky spires hidden in rain or raking out above clouds and land and green. The winds blew hard against us, unbroken by trees, and we followed the little stone cairns that marked the trail above tree line in place of the white blazes. On the way up Lafayette, Jones and I stopped for a break. Squirrel was behind, as he always was in the morning. Sitting and eating gorp, I noticed a small gray and white bird eyeing me passionately. The bird's expression was not so much different from the puppy eyes my little brown dog back home wore whenever I held food in my hand. I felt a swell of longing for my faraway companion. Placing a few pieces of the gorp in my palm I held it out and up. The bird fluttered instantly to me and perched cautiously on the tips of my bare fingers. The little talons gripped with the gentle tenacity and balance of a dancing spider. The bird was impossibly light as it pecked the little bits of grain from the small of my palm. Then there were more birds watching us and Jones joined in, holding out a handful of gorp to be sampled. As Squirrel caught up to join us, we stood in a halo of fluttering birds.

The White Mountains are maintained by the Appalachian Mountain Club (or AMC), also known among hikers as the Appalachian Money Club. They had a lot of rules about where hikers could camp, and most of them made a lot of sense. Vegetation above tree line is very sensitive and slow growing, and camping on it would surely destroy it so there was no camping allowed above tree line. Since much of the trail in the Whites stays above tree line, the hikers mostly have to stay in the huts that are maintained like primitive little hotels. The AMC got its nickname by charging fifty dollars per night to stay in the huts. This sum was substantially more than any hiker would consider paying simply for trying to follow the rules. The huts were rustic little resorts offering walls, windows, light, toilets, and meals. They were primarily filled with tourists and vacationers used to paying outrageous sums for a bed, and in the summer months when the thru-hikers were passing the Whites, it was the peak tourist season. The huts did offer to let some hikers work off their stay, but sometimes huts were full or there wasn't enough work for more than a couple, and they would ask the hikers to pay or move on. It seemed criminal since it might be six more miles over barren rock through blasting, frigid winds in the growing dark to the next legal camping spot. Some hut "croos" were more humane than others, but others treated thru-hikers like vagrants, or ordinary tourists who just didn't want to pay. Even if we did get a chance to work for food and lodging, we couldn't eat until after all the paying guests ate. Then we had to help the croo clean up the tables before being given the cold scraps left over from the guests' meals. It was rarely enough to feed a hungry hiker. In the mornings we would have to work for a few hours, losing some of the best hiking time of the day.

The night after climbing Lafayette, we stayed in Galehead hut. The croo wasn't sure they had enough work for the Vikings and the other two thru-hikers that were there but found small tasks for us all to complete so that they could let everyone stay. They also let us complete our tasks in the evening so we could get an early start in the morning, and when the leftovers from dinner came up short, they brought out some extra crackers and Fig Newtons to make sure we weren't left starving. We stayed up late after our meal talking and sharing stories of the trail with the hut croo. Two new hikers that we met while hut-hopping were Jake and Willwood, a pair called the Blues Brothers. Jake was short and stocky and pulled his hair back in a short ponytail. Will was tall and lanky with a perpetual grin. Both were quick to laugh and funny as could be. There was no question they would get along with the Vikings.

During our dinner in the kitchen, Beorn had also come bellowing in, looking for food and explaining his status as a yo-yoer and not a thru-hiker to the staff. The croo, however, had received radio transmissions about the volume of his infamous snoring from the last hut where Beorn stayed. They asked him to sleep on the porch since none of the paying guests at the last hut had slept at all the night before and there had been many complaints. Beorn was vocally upset and hiked off into the dark. We had seen Beorn every now and then since he caught up to us at Delaware Water Gap for the church feast. The stories of his yellow-blazing and other adventures had only grown since Trail Days. It seemed that everyone had another story about the giant. Most popular were the stories that involved insinuation that he wasn't actually doing much hiking. The most commonly presented pieces of evidence were that he wore flimsy sandals that never deteriorated under his massive frame, and no matter how long he "hiked" he never lost any weight. Back in Massachusetts we had even run into a pair of reporters from *Outside Magazine* who were looking for Beorn. Whatever the stories, the hut croo that had been so understanding and kind to us turned him out.

Later in our bunks, Squirrel looked in one of the bird books in the hut to find out what kind of bird it was that had fluttered about us earlier in the day so he could record it in his journal. Finding the markings he read the description of the bird aloud.

"The Canadian Jay is a scavenger that will eat out of your hand and even perch on your lip and eat out of your mouth."

"Great," I said, "we were just tourists. My magical moment is shot, and I gave that little bastard some of my food! He totally duped me! They're just flying mice!"

New Hampshire was Squirrel's stomping ground and he had friends all around the Whites. Every few days someone would meet us at a road crossing where the mountains dropped out of the sky and take us home with him to eat dinner, listen to music, and sleep in beds before returning to the trail with the sunrise. We wandered through the Presidentials from one majestic peak to the next, following the stone cairns on our winding way over, between, and around the mountains, occasionally dipping into woods and valleys. We crossed the famous Mount Washington on a perfect day when visibility was a hundred miles or more, but there were so many tourists on top, having ridden the cog railway or driven up the steep road in a car, that we hurried off the crowded and polluted summit. The air tasted like the back of a bus from the car exhaust and the billowing black smoke that poured off the cog railway. On the way down the mountain the train slowly chugged by, dishing out inky puffs of stench. We improvised a dramatic death scene where we collapsed, clutching our throats for the confused and disturbed audience on the cog. Before we left New Hampshire, we caught up to Kaptain Krummholz on Wildcat Mountain. He was feeling terribly ill, and we carted him back down the mountain to one of Squirrel's friend's houses for a day off so that we could continue together when he was well. Jake and Willwood also joined us, opting for new fellowship.

The places Squirrel's friends would take us were very different from the short hitches to the restaurants and post offices near the trail we were accustomed to. The service people in trail towns were used to hikers, had grown accustomed to our pacing, our distance and tendencies. After so many months in the woods, our spirits loomed expectantly over each moment like a little boy crouched over a centipede. Farther from the trail, people handled our moments roughly, without consideration, sending their conversations one way, their minds another, their bodies jittery and unbalanced. We avoided them in self defense. I had noticed during these side trips and even on the long breaks at Squirrel's house that I remained Wayah and a Viking almost exclusively. When things didn't fit, I wouldn't revert to my mind before the trail to work them out, but simply push through for better or worse.

Before entering Maine and leaving civilized places for the remainder of our hike, we indulged Squirrelfight's love for cold hamburger lunches one last time. The night before we left, Squirrel's friends drove us miles from the trail to a McDonalds where we could eat our fill inexpensively and stock up on burgers for the next day. The other Vikings had already navigated through the cashier and gone to sit down with their food when I realized that it was my turn to approach the hard, smooth counter. Because they would sit in backpacks overnight, any sandwiches with mayo on them had to be eaten for dinner, but the rest could be carried with no trouble. The fluorescent lighting and the unsteady manner of the cashier immediately put me on my guard. I reminded myself of the way transactions like this were supposed to go and rehearsed it once in my head before taking the step forward.

"I'll have two Big Macs, three hamburgers, and three cheeseburgers." I spoke very clearly and then eyed the cashier appraisingly. I was looking forward to dropping down into the soft, curved booth with my friends to eat, but I didn't like the way the cashier started poking at his machine without looking at me. There was a sudden sideways glance and then he spun to grab three of the sandwiches. He seemed to feint one way and then bounce back the other and I realized that I was jerking lightly with his movements. He breezed by, dropping some of the food on a tray and mumbled the price of the food, smiling as he said it, but he never looked at me, and the vacant space of his eyes filled me with dread. I was already holding out more than enough money to cover the sum glowing red in the hollow window of the register, but he didn't take it and spun around again, leaving me wondering what was going wrong. I was rehearsing it again when I realized he had taken the money and I took a reflexive step back. He quickly counted out bills and change onto the counter and I leaned over to grab them and the large bag of sandwiches that I assumed was full since he had stopped moving. I pocketed the change and prepared to return to better company when I felt his eyes lock on me for the first time. Mine snapped magnetically to his and I turned back to him, ready. He was holding up two pennies, one tarnished and one sparkling new.

"Is it all right if I don't give you these two pennies?" he said. The two pennies hung there in front of me like little poles of age and youth, a story of impermanence. I had no particular fondness for pennies, and change in general was not something we wanted to carry around with us, but whatever was going on here obviously involved elements that I couldn't quite grasp. His look, which had begun with a certain calm that I hadn't expected, was turning to a more challenging posture. I broke away from his gaze and quickly glanced at the change already in my hand and made a vain attempt to count it all before deciding I must have heard the boy wrong and locked eyes with him again.

"What?" I grinned a big fake grin, afraid that my nerves would get the best of me. I could feel the dizzying net of contracts, obligations, assumptions, and niceties fluttering around me, and I both desired its embrace to push me out of this encounter and also feared its hold.

"Is it all right if I don't give you these two pennies?" he asked again, a replay of the first in every way. Sweat broke on my brow. I could feel my body trying to kick in to fight or flight mode as I looked at the boy taunting me with the enigmatic two pennies. I suppressed the urge to dive over the counter and knock the pennies from his hand and gathered myself together enough to speak. Attempting to assert my dominance through my gaze I spoke slowly."I think you should do whatever you think is right."

I watched his reaction closely while backing away, praying he wouldn't say anything else and watching for him to call the Rangers or the Police, but he just dropped his gaze, shaking his head as he returned the pennies to the register and began skittering about again.

Walking to the booth where the Vikings were eating quietly, I felt very exposed in the fluorescent lighting. As I thought over the encounter I puzzled that the cashier may have been the *normal* one, and I was overcome by a profound sorrow that the end of the trail was so near and that this was what was waiting for me at its end. Squirrel looked up at me and then down again and slapped the table,

"Damn it! I forgot to ask them to leave off the pickles and add extra love! Dah, now I have to start all over again. I'll wear my sunglasses this time so I don't arouse any suspicion." He walked back to the counter giggling to himself.

CHAPTER 13

Monson, Maine
2,050 miles down and 118 miles to go

Carl Newhall Shelter:
A delightful hike here today - a beautiful (sunny, cool, windless) day for hiking. GREAT to see Sulu again and meet Father Time and Huck. And of course, it was a delight to see Campro for the first time since we got cut off at Brownie's in Delaware Water Gap (I'm still bitter about that). I have abandoned my laissez-faire attitude toward purists; today I personally drowned three of them in Cloud Pond. I hope they don't struggle to the surface and come after me with their ski poles. OH AND BY THE WAY - are you tired of Southbound section hikers who pretend they know EVERYTHING there is to know about the trail? If so, please consider spearing one with a tent peg. You'll be making the trail a nicer place. You won't have to hear about what a brutal climb Nesuntabunt Mountain is, you won't have to suffer through uninformed discussions about the AMC. Visions of the perfect world.

The Ordainer
GA > Perfection

We had been writing "Georgia to Maine" in the registers for almost six months, and now we were crossing the state line into that last stretch of trail. We still had over 300 miles and almost a month to go, but it seemed like only a few steps and a few days. The long fold-out map of the trail that I had carried since Hot Springs was now a story of where we had been instead of

140

a lengthy reminder of how far we had to go. There were only a few inches left on the map, and at the end of the dotted red line was a small National Park punctuated by Mt. Katahdin. "K-Town," we had been calling it. "The Big K." The Whites had been monumental, and now we were in Maine's rugged lake country. We had heard stories about Maine all along the way, and now the objects of the stories were only miles or tens of miles away.

Back in North Carolina we had passed Knothole Willie and Wolf Cloud, who were finishing a long southbound thru-hike that had taken them all the way through the winter. Willie told us about Mahoosuc Notch, the hardest mile on the trail, and the climb that came after it. He said, "The Notch is the crotch, but the Arm does the harm." Now we descended into the infamous boulder-strewn gap, gleefully leaping and climbing, scrambling and sliding to where Mahoosuc Arm shot steep and high out of the gorge.

We came to the infamous Kennebec River, eighty feet across with no bridge. The old tradition of fording the river on foot had been replaced by a manned canoe to ferry people across after some hikers died. The danger of the river was that if you slipped and your pack got wet, it would instantly triple in weight and hold you down on the bottom—plus there were flood gates far up stream that opened and closed on an irregular schedule. The ferry was technically optional, but the ATC demanded its use, saying one of the blazes was in the boat. The thru-hikers still talked about fording the wide river, though. For some it was bravado, for others tradition, but I was undecided. I didn't fear falling in so much, but people talking was no basis for making a decision. I had to see it for myself. I was the first Viking on the scene, having left camp early that morning. I looked at the canoe and some section hikers climbing in and looked at the river. It occurred to me that I could just take the canoe and not have to dry my boots for hours, not to mention the risk of falling in. Lately a pebble-sized paranoia had set in. One bad step and I could break an ankle or a knee and would have to crawl or limp the rest of the way to Katahdin. I looked at the water flowing smoothly here, roughly there, and at the round, slippery rocks along the bottom. They were like greased bowling balls, shiny with algae and fish funk. I heard Jones coming up behind me. The morning sun shone hard and cut the river valley in stark, contrasting shapes.

"You takin' the canoe?" Jones asked from behind. As usual, hearing the question from another Viking helped me quickly make up my mind. I had been in a canoe before, but I had never forded a river like this one.

"Hell, no. I'm fordin' this big lady." Jones gave a triumphant laugh as I picked up my gear and looked for the best place to cross. I unhooked the belt strap on the pack, letting it hang on my shoulders so that I could quickly get out of it if the river pulled it down, and found a fairly shallow area to start from. It was wider, but punctuated by a sandbar in the middle, and I began to make my way slowly across the tumbling, slippery rocks. The instant my boots entered the water, I felt the river start to intrude on my normally watertight foot-fortress. Within seconds the boots were filled with frigid water—so cold my feet quickly became numb clubs. This was another challenge of crossing this way no one had mentioned. I crossed the wide river slowly, propped up by my walking stick and leaning upstream into the powerful current, placing my legs deliberately and commanding my muscles by sight instead of feel. The water was up to my shorts and pulling hard against me. Jones was right behind, using two sticks from beside the river to aid his balance. From the mountain approach, Squirrel saw us crossing, and he and Krummholz trotted down to begin their own ford. When the ferryman finished porting the section hikers and saw that we were crossing on foot he jumped from his seat and readied his rescue rope to toss to us if we were to suddenly go down and float by him. Despite some dicey balance moments on the rounded slick rocks, though, none of us fell in. Once across, we sat in the sun by the tiny Caratunk general store and post office for two hours, drying our boots in the sun, eating fresh, sweet cucumber that the ferryman had offered us, and opening mail drops with the other hikers that had crossed since we arrived.

Each day was like an entire chapter in our adventure. Each mountain and lake seemed the last of its kind and we were more present to each moment and alert to each detail than ever before as the end crept closer. We traveled on and off with Just Chris, Rainman, and Johnny Stick. They were all good camp companions and Jones loved to play cards with them, sometimes stopping right on the trail to do so. The Blues Brothers hiked with us most every day, and camped with us often. Some nights the Viking horde numbered nine, and when Krummholz's friend Ledgehead joined us after Caratunk to hike the last stretch to Katahdin, we were ten. We were seeing more thru-hikers than we had ever seen in the woods before. When we started, we were ahead of the crowd, but now, with October drawing near, we were finally in the main flow. In mid-October, Katahdin would become too dangerous to climb, and at whatever point the winds and ice became deadly, the park would have to be closed. So everyone was aiming to finish by the end of September or in the first few days of October to be certain that they would be allowed to finish at all. Several hikers also had friends and family come out to join them for the end of their journey. Rolling into a camp site, we might find it packed with twenty or thirty people. Not interested in such a crowd, we would stay back or move ahead to find some water we could camp by and be alone. After a while, even ten was too many, and Chris, Rainman, and Stick would camp separately, and sometimes Jones with them.

In Monson, all of us but the Kaptain and Ledgehead shared a house that could be rented for the day for forty dollars. Monson would be our last trail town and our last re-supply. In the mail we all got huge packages of food to get us through the next ten days. Monson lay at the southern edge of the Hundred Mile Wilderness. For one hundred miles there would be no places to re-supply, and only a few little dirt roads trailing off into the green. Our travel arrangements for the end of the trail had stayed flexible before now so that we wouldn't have to set our pace by a hard schedule, but now we had to set a date to be picked up from the foot of Katahdin. We could send back anything that we wouldn't need, and we had to fill our packs to the brim with food one more time. The end of the trail was staring us in the face. It was said that you could see Katahdin sticking out of the land like a pillar for days before you got there. We soaked up our last trail town as best we could. We dried and cleaned all our gear, did laundry, and took a final shower. We prepared a feast with everything we could find in the tiny town store and celebrated into the night.

By morning a light rain had settled in and Jones wasn't feeling well. He decided to sit the day out with Stick, Rainman, and Chris. Squirrel and I and the Blues Brothers caught a ride in the back of a truck through the stinging rain to the trailhead and dove back into the forest. I was glad to have my heavy fleece and thick jacket back in the past weeks. The days were turning cold and keeping heat in with the heavier raincoat was becoming essential. The nights were often frigid, and we woke up in the morning to find beads of ice on the insides of our tents. That first night it rained hard all night. Squirrel and I had fallen behind the Blues Brothers, the Kaptain, and Ledgehead and had camped on an unused road by a river that the others had already passed. We didn't want to start a river crossing after the sun had set. Besides the danger, we did not like the idea of not having any sunlight to dry off our boots on the other side. That night the driving rain streamed down the steep road and soaked us inside our tents. Our food bags were saturated where they hung, and some of my candy bars and gorp bag were filled with water. A long time ago we had learned to laugh off getting soaked. What gets wet in the rain dries as soon as the sun comes out. We took a long lunch the next day on a rocky outcropping to dry our gear. Even my wet trail mix in its new brick-form would not go to waste.

Squirrel was given some military-issue camouflage face-paint by a friend while he was at home during his Harper's Ferry break. He had carried it all those months without using it. Now, in the Hundred Mile Wilderness, we decided we would wear it every day, and it became the Viking Warpaint. We caught the Blues Brothers, Kaptain Krummholz, and Ledgehead the next evening at the shelter, and the next day Jones, Chris, Rainman, and Stick caught up and they all began wearing the Warpaint every day in the Wilderness. If the dread locks and Warpaint weren't enough, Squirrel was wearing a skirt he had picked up at a New Hampshire flea market. He said it provided him more freedom and ventilation, but we suspected it was to frighten section-hikers. We marched through the Hundred Mile Wilderness in a long, strung-out, painted line, seeing old faces and new ones. We even saw Jokers Wild bouncing through the Wilderness in different directions, hitching a ride back to Monson with a prop-plane that landed on a trailside lake. The terrain became mild as we came out of the higher mountains into the lake country. We wound around water and climbed a few mountains, but the rugged climbs of New Hampshire and southern Maine were basically behind us.

At the end of any good climb we would squint intently at the horizon for signs of Katahdin. It seemed like it would glow, but we were rarely sure if one of the mountains we saw in the distance was our goal. We sat on cliffs on many days eating lunch and taking long breaks, staring at the horizon. Food was dwindling more than we would have liked even after a few days. The desire to eat some of the weight off of our overloaded packs combined with the cold weather was bringing our appetites to a peak, and halfway through we were already having to ration to make sure we didn't run out of food before the store at Abol Bridge on the other side of the Wilderness. The store was probably small and wouldn't have many of our usual staples, but it became apparent that we would have to completely restock there for the last two days, even if it meant eating nothing but gas station junk food.

I sat with the assembled Vikings on a high cliff one day during a break, jesting and snacking. Krummholz was eating peanut butter and bread and laughing. We had never stopped having fun, but now we were euphoric. Jones was even able to move back and forth between different groups of Vikings when stress crept up on him, but with the end almost literally in sight, his spirits remained high. From the clear sky swooped several Canadian Jays. After our experience in the Whites they looked like little Vultures, craning their necks, hopping closer to our food like tiny thieves. Krummholz kicked out at one half-jokingly and then screamed as the joke turned tragic. His jerking leg had brushed against his jar of peanut butter and knocked it off the ledge. Some two thousand calories, one hundred sixty grams of fat, and seventy grams of protein bounced hard down the rocky face of the cliff, catching in some brush twenty or thirty feet below. We all stared over the cliff in hungry torment.

"Wow," I said, shocked. "That really sucks." Krummholz half laughed, half whimpered to himself.

"I can't let this go," Squirrel suddenly blurted out. "That peanut butter's in a shatterproof container. I'm going after it." We wanted to tell him he was mad, but we couldn't argue his reasoning, and besides, the Viking Hero was already scrambling down the cliff face.

"You better not fall," I called down. "I don't want to have to carry your ass all the way up Katahdin!" He did not fall, though, and true to his name, he rescued the peanut butter amid genuine applause.

One day I crested a small ridge and saw Rainman and Jones standing transfixed and looking into the distance, their packs still on. It was there, like the White Whale gliding out of the fog that hung over the plains. There was no question and no squinting: it was

Katahdin. We gathered in a row amid the brush and rock as the rest of the Vikings arrived, faces painted and serene, and stared for longer than we knew. Each day it was bigger, closer. We saw it coming over Nesuntabunt Mountain like a great dragon, the veins of rock running down her steep sides clear in the cold air. We camped by a dam on the edge of Rainbow Lake, and she stood over the trees and reflected in the water, greeting us with the sunrise as geese flew over in formation, their wings rushing in the wind. The end marched ever closer, and then what? What would it be like to live in that world out there again, where my routines no longer made so much sense, where the day was measured in unbreakable moments instead of flexible experiences, where weather was an afterthought instead of the thing that shaped the way I went about my days. I remembered the person I had been before the trail and wondered what part of my new life would survive leaving the woods. Going back to school and work, paying bills, having to ask for permission to disappear for a few days alone—it was big and frightening. I had found a life of blissful adventure in the simplicity of the trail, and I didn't know how I could just leave it. Even during the hardest times on the trail, the clarity of our dilemmas and hurts were more than countered by our equally simple and more powerful joys. Our lives had been boiled down to simple questions with simple answers. Where will I sleep? What will I eat? What makes me happy? In the world off the trail there were too many answers to these questions, so many conflicts that every choice inevitably wound up violating another priority, and answers broke into long strings and balancing acts that caused as much stress as relief. Perhaps our gentle simplicity came from depending on no one but ourselves in the woods, but once off the trail we would be stuck in the tangled web again of people too many to count intertwined in our support and struggle. I began to fill my contemplative moments with thoughts about how I could apply what I had learned in the woods to the life I would have to live when I was out of it. Our fears surfaced as humor, of course. Sentimentality was tolerated only three times per person per day. Any more and the offender would be covered with a sleeping bag and beaten. Even just a sigh followed by a vocalization of the number of days left to Katahdin counted as an offense. I thought about the Wolf and what he had taught me. I considered that he was me, that I was not learning but uncovering. I practiced with Brooke's juggling balls, and remembered how it felt to get off the bus, to follow my instincts and plunge into the unknown. Mostly I enjoyed my friends with every ounce of attention I could muster, chronicled their laughter, and reveled in our perfectly balanced and simple support of one another.

Before we knew it we were crossing Abol Bridge, the end of the Hundred Mile Wilderness. After leaving the store there were only fifteen miles left to the top of Katahdin. The heavy metal bridge lay draped across the Penobscot River like some girded vessel and along its side was a walkway for hikers. When I got there, Jones, Chris, Stick, and Rainman were already sitting in a line on the railing. Over the wide, winding Penobscot sat Katahdin. It was only a few miles away by the crow and stood monolithic over us. The days had been beautiful, the odd hailstorm aside, and now the air was crisp and the mountain held the deep blue sky high above us. It was September twenty eighth. We weren't due to meet our respective rides at the foot of Katahdin until the first of October. We would spend the night at the campground by the bridge, have a leisurely walk eight miles the next day to the Daicey Pond campground, and then that night we would climb the mountain.

When I was fourteen, long before I ever knew of the trail, I had gone to a summer camp in Maine. I had never hiked, but I liked mountains and had decided to join a three-day field trip to climb Katahdin. I had been intoxicated by its majesty then, even though it was covered with clouds that day and I could only see about twenty feet. I had looked on curiously as two ragged

Frenchmen staggered through the mist to the top with heavy packs and looks of indescribable joy. It was years and years before I realized that they must have been thru-hikers and that the first mountain I had climbed was the end of the Appalachian Trail. I remembered the group leader saying that Katahdin, as the tallest mountain in the eastern-most state, was the first place the sun hit in America in the morning, and when I put it all together I knew that I had to hike that whole trail and watch that sunrise from the top. Along the way I had shared my plan and aroused some excitement among fellow hikers. Some had tried to tell me that the first place the sun hit was some other mountain farther to the east in Maine, but I was always able to convince them of the truth.

The next day we woke up and had a leisurely day. I bought a box of Fruit Loops and a half gallon of milk and ate them for breakfast. Squirrel had chocolate-filled doughnuts. We saw Screaming Coyote for the first time since Vermont as he hiked in early from the shelter, and we proceeded slowly on our way. It was only eight miles to the Daicey Pond campground and we had plenty of time to relax. We took long breaks to talk and snack, and then took lunch at the Little Niagara Falls. Squirrel and Ledgehead had crossed the low falls, surveying the slope of the water as it cascaded a few feet into the stream below to determine if it would be safe to slide down. Willwood was trying to cross the slippery top of the falls to join them and was not faring well in the current. For each timid step he took forward with a long, lanky leg, he would slide a few inches toward the edge. Krummholz and I sat on the trailside in the sun, shaking our heads saying, "Nope. I don't think he's gonna make it." Suddenly Willwood turned down the waterfall and dove in head first, laughing in compliance with the will of the falls. Squirrel and Ledgehead were close behind.

We reached Daicey early and had a lot of time to look around and see who was there after we had been registered and informed of the park rules. The reporters were all there. All the teams had gathered to hike the end together, and we were able to see many faces that we hadn't seen in a long time. Harper's Fairy and Curly had just come down off the mountain and were heading for town. Screaming Coyote was there with his parents who were so excited they could barely acknowledge anyone else in the world. Saprophite was camped with her new man, Peace Dog, and the campground was filled with hikers barely known and strangers never met. Many people, the reporters especially, had food and soda and beer to give us, and we talked and rejoiced with our friends into the evening. After dark we went out on the pond in canoes and circled in the dark, whistling across the water.

We were ready for our night hike. Squirrel, Jones, Krummholz, Ledgehead, Jake, Will, and I would hike to the ranger's hut at the base of the mountain and leave our packs on the ranger's porch. Then we would hike up for the sunrise with just lamps, water, and snacks, and have the top to ourselves before hiking down the other side over the Knife's Edge to meet our families at the Roaring Brook campground. Then we could be driven back around to the ranger's station to get the rest of our things. We decided to get in a few hours of sleep before midnight, though, and set up our sleeping bags in a field by the full campground. So the Vikings wouldn't oversleep, I kept watch over them in the night instead of napping. I didn't feel tired, and my mind was churning. The end had come so quickly. Each day that I spent with my friends I numbered among the best days in my life. There was a kind of energy that hovered around the Vikings, making the world magical and forcing everyone in its field to comply with our joy. I built myself a small fire and sat looking into it and listening to its crackling, waving flames. I knew I would survive the world on the other side, but where would that energy go once the Vikings had scattered across the country again? The hours crawled by slowly in the cold air, and I was serene, surrounded by my sleeping friends, keeping a silent vigil.

CHAPTER 14

Mount Katahdin, Baxter State Park, Maine
2,168 miles

"Blackbird singin' in the dead of night, take these broken wings and learn to fly. All your life you have only waited for this moment to arise. Blackbird, fly into the light of the dark black night."

John Lennon/Paul McCartney

At midnight I put out my little fire and started nudging the scattered sleeping bags as the Vikings quietly began to stir. We packed up our bags and gear and put on all our layers of clothing; the night air had turned frigid while the Vikings slept. Some put on the Viking Warpaint. I pulled out the mask I had found on my birthday in Oswego, the red-brown leather face bearing the scowl of the Wolf, and tied the leather straps loosely behind my head. We slid over the two miles to Katahdin Stream campground and stopped to make hot tea before dropping our packs. The criss-crossed beams of the headlamps lit the steam as it rose from the pot over the stove, and we drank the tea and filled water bottles with the steaming liquid and looked at the map one last time before stuffing it into a pack. Katahdin was like a great wall on the profile map. It was the steepest, toughest climb on the whole trail and the profile map had an extra fold out three times the regular height to record it. The climb was 4,200 feet of vertical gain, most of it in the first three miles, and we were going to tackle it in the dark. We quietly leaned our packs inside the ranger's porch, but he woke up anyway and ambled into the night trying to show more authority than weariness.

"It's a little late for a midnight hike, don't you think?" the ranger boomed, shattering the silence.

"Actually," I said, checking my watch through my mask, "it's the perfect time. We'd best be movin' on."

The Mountain embraced us like its children. Our bodies were heating up from the climb and the woods wrapped around us, shadows dancing in the weaving lights. We stopped briefly for a drink where the trail broke away from Katahdin Stream and then continued on in single file, saying little. Up and up we climbed, the trail steep and jagged. We had to use our hands often, and scrambled up sheer faces, trying not to slide down on top of each other or kick off any loose rocks. Whoever was leading would stop on a ledge for a moment to catch his breath and let everyone catch up, so we stayed in a tight group throughout the climb. The night was cold, but occasionally a balmy wind would blow down the face of the mountain carrying warm air from some faraway tropical land.

Halfway up we broke out above tree line. We could see to the sides as far as our lights would reach, and all around us was rock. Clear stars lit the clean fabric of night and ended in a great arc of black where the Mountain waited above us. Now the climb was all on rock. From boulder to boulder we scrambled and leaped, always up, sometimes so steeply there were metal bars drilled into the stone to grab on to. I found myself in front and from time to time I would stop and turn off my light. Behind me I saw the trail of six headlamps weaving up the rocky slope. As I turned the light back on, the rocks for a few feet around me were lit, and beyond them the world trailed off into cold darkness and sky. The wind blew coolly across the rock face, refreshing us as we grew hotter from the continual climb. We had worried that the night climb would be dangerously cold, but the temperature couldn't have been more perfect. We climbed hand over hand as if the mountain was a play structure, and each new rock was a puzzle to be grappled with.

Then the rock leveled. The climb up the mountain face was over and we emerged onto the Table Lands that sloped gently up to the top. We had less than two miles to go. In front, I could see the eastern sky beginning to slip from black to dark blue, a halo of color breaking the night, and in the center of it, the peak of the mountain stuck up as if it were the source of that dimmest of lights. Behind I could see the silhouettes of my friends winding along the rock-strewn plain, their lights dancing at their feet. The procession moved quickly, hopping over the rocks as they appeared out of the black and watching the sky ahead grow slowly brighter. The stars that crowned the mountain's approaching peak started to fade.

Contrast grew in the cracks between the rocks as dawn approached and I turned off my headlamp, picking my way toward the top as my eyes adjusted to the dimness through my mask. Ahead I could see the silhouette of the wooden sign that was imprinted in my head from so many photos on the walls of post offices or trail stations. It was barely distinct from the tangled rocks of the slope, but the shape was so hauntingly familiar as to be unmistakable. It was the end. I turned on my light and read the old, weather-beaten planks. We had passed hundreds of wooden signs with arrows pointing forward and backwards down the trail, giving distances to the next spring, road, or shelter, but all the arrows on this sign pointed back the way we came.

KATAHDIN
Baxter Peak - Elevation - 5267 ft.
Northern Terminus of the
Appalachian Trail
A Mountain Footpath Extending Over
2000 Miles to Springer Mtn. Georgia
< Thoreau Spring 1.0m.
< Katahdin Stream Campground 5.2

< Penobscot West Branch at Abol Bridge 14.5
< Maine - New Hampshire State Line 274.0
< Mt. Washington, N. H. 323.6
< Springer Mtn., Georgia 2135.0

Behind me came the other Vikings, stopping in silence to see the sign and to think their own thoughts. The view from Katahdin was more beautiful than we could have dreamed. On the horizon the blues that drifted into the starry sky were growing bright, and edges of purple and pink were giving way to reds and oranges. We gathered there on top, silent but for the quiet congratulations and warm embraces. Our giddiness was overcome with quiet admiration as we sank into the landscape and waited for those first rays of the sun. The sky grew ever brighter, drowning the stars and casting light down into the valleys that swam in milky lakes of mist. The minutes went by with all our eyes fixed tightly on the horizon, waiting for that first speck of light as the mountain we had blindly scaled slowly revealed itself below us. The megalithic rocks dropped sharply to the lake far below, the walls veined with the gashes and wrinkles of the teeth and claws of glaciers and countless years. To either side, like the bowed wings of an angel, stretched the arms of Katahdin, the wide and flat Table Land from which we had come, and the narrow jagged path of the Knife Edge where we would descend when we saw the masses approaching the summit. Each moment I thought the sun would appear, longed for it, dreaded it. With the sun my adventure would be complete, whole, perfect, finished, only memories.

Then it jumped the horizon: a pinprick of brilliant white and fire that began slowly to unfold. We put our hands up high and felt those first rays on our fingertips. On October 1st, 1995, the sun slid over the ocean to find Vikings waiting on the summit of that most beautiful of mountains.

I untied the straps that held the leather mask to my face and slid down to a seat among the rocks, setting the wolf gently in my lap. The cold wind that curled across the summit caught the thin layer of sweat that had gathered under the mask during the climb, and my face felt alive, exposed. I looked around at my friends smiling and at peace, watching the sun, still slipping gently out of the mist. For hours we sat there with the sun's warmth cutting through the hard breeze, filling the sky with an unwavering blue, igniting the wispy clouds that drifted above and beyond us. Surely there has never been a peace as pure as those hours when we sat on the earth's throne, kings and children, watching the world turn around us.

EPILOGUE

When we spied the specks of hikers and reporters scrambling across the Table Land, we left the summit and the white blazes. The Knife's Edge danced up and down, the trail along its edge one of the most exciting sections we had hiked yet, with sharp climbs up and down over jagged trail with steep drop-offs on both sides, but it was no longer *the* trail. Though we hiked with our usual enthusiasm, there was a vulnerability to each of our moments. We weren't heading for camp or the next spring; we were following blue blazes to a parking lot where cars and family waited with food and drinks and congratulations. From there we would go in different directions from each other, and back to the unchanging world where we suddenly felt like strangers.

We lingered as long as we could in the parking lot before saying goodbye to Jones, the Kaptain, Jake and Willwood. I went back to Squirrel's house for a few days to await the plane ride that would take me back to Atlanta where I would drive my car home to Little Rock. I tried to get used to calling him Jonny instead of Squirrel, but didn't like it and decided to give it more time. We tried to get used to driving a car, but the car moved so fast, everyone was so agitated and hurried, and our feet were still numb. We tried to get used to eating normal amounts of food, but our metabolisms were set to a long day of labor and would take weeks to reset. We finally parted with knowing smiles, wished each other luck with the world and knew it would not be too long before our trails crossed again.

Atlanta brought me back to civilization with a jolt. The compounded smells and noises traffic, franchise, and frantic urgency bit far more deeply than the unwieldy adjustments to Squirrel's little town in New Hampshire. I found that my car, which had been sitting for six and a half months, would not start. I was so far from the trail. This piece of gear I could not fix. I knew of others that could, but their connection to me was based on my money, and they would take all they could. I was looking for the simplicity of the trail mirrored in the busy world off of it, but that world was vastly more clouded, involved so many more people, demanded so many more decisions and considerations to reach the same point.

I returned home, to school and study, to my house and dog and bed, my friends from the trail so far away that only an airplane or days in a car would bring me to them. Life settled back in and routine enveloped my days—working, paying bills, eating on schedule, exercising intentionally, and having to arrange vacations in order to attempt uncluttered days. Even vacations did not compare to the clarity of my time on the AT, though. A couple of times in the months following the trail, I had to run away spontaneously and travel aimlessly, but as the feeling in my feet returned, my appetite returned to normal, and the pace of my life resumed, I began slowly to fit back into the web.

As enveloped in the tapestry of modern life as I've become, the trail is never far from my mind. I have a head full of stories and lifelong friends that may be far away in body but never in spirit, and whose memories of the trail are just as fresh. We are always only a word away from the potluck, the mountaintop, the endless laughter, and the unfettered simplicity of our shared thoughts. The Wolf is always with me even if he whispers more than howls. He keeps those powerful images clear in my mind whenever I am tempted to doubt or fear. His visions are so sharp and enveloping that I can return to that moment just after getting off the bus and feel the electric vibrancy of throwing my entire lot into the unknown. Without this fearlessness, I would never have been able to leave my job of eight years and start the business of my dreams. I can see Coyote's face as he asked for help with his water bottle and know that I am not my body, and physical ills that may affect my daily routine do not affect my spirit. Those and a hundred other moments inform my life and surround it, and because I was so entirely present to each experience, they are easier to step back into and relive than memories from off the trail.

I kept in close contact with the Vikings in the years following the trail, and especially with Squirrelfight. The year following our end-to-end hike he spent the summer in Arkansas where we poured through journals, developed photos in the dark room, and hiked all the trails we could find. Squirrel and Kaptain Krummholz settled in San Francisco where Squirrel became the most knowledgeable Manager of a Ben and Jerry's franchise ever, and the Kaptain returned to building props and museum exhibits, and planning our next great adventure. We planned to hike the Pacific Crest Trail in 2000, but by the time it came around, Jones was settled into his new career in pharmaceuticals in Colorado, and I had met my wife and my hiking money had gone into our new life. I had to settle for being the support team for my friends, now known as the Menacing Vegetables, as they navigated the west coast from Mexico to Canada, missing them every step of their adventure, and loving my new married life.

Squirrelfight gradually became Jonny. He and Maria, whom he had dated since shortly after hiking the A.T. and had hiked the Pacific Crest with him as *Pickle*, lived in the woods near Seattle for years after their P.C.T. hike, working as maintainers at a Hot Springs they had discovered along the way. Once they had saved up enough money they moved to Bellingham, Washington where they started a business delivering organic produce to people's door. They got married and stared making baby boys a few years after I did.

Kaptain Krummholz, who gradually became Ben, eventually married Rachel, who had hiked much of the P.C.T. with the Vegetables, and she and Ben continued on to adventure through South America for many more months before returning to the States, where Ben went to architecture school and now practices in San Francisco.

Jones became Bevans, and still lives in Colorado where he is an avid mountain-biker and cyclocross racer. He and his wife adopted a son from China and Bevans always speaks of their life with the same mixture of abundant enthusiasm and lightly reigned pride that we grew to love in the woods.

As the years tick by, we see each other less as our lives become thicker and richer, and the miles between us seem darker and harder to penetrate. If not before, we always talk or send a note on October first. My first son was born on that anniversary of the Viking summit of Katahdin, and we gave him the name Wayah, hoping the wolf would speak to him all his life. His birthday is a day of reflection for me. Hearing the words of my old friends, remembering my masks, and thinking over the lyrics of my life like the day I found my trail name always reminds me how much I was changed, but how far away from the blazes I've made my trail.

Every spring, when the cold air begins to lilt with the muddy warmth of rhododendron and the dewy lure of honeysuckle, my thoughts go back to the trail. Not a year goes by that I don't hear the Wolf stirring the leaves, feel those days come back to me in all their passion and laughter and strength, remind myself of how simple and unfettered life can be, and wonder when I'll have my next adventure. The sun on a field or a breeze through the trees can bring it all back, as can the unencumbered laughter of my friends.

What is this life if not a long trail, where we push toward our known and unknown goals and pause for a moment of perfect awareness where the earth drops away into beauty? We are aware of the ups and downs, but rarely the direction of our movement. When we are at our lowest and cannot hold ourselves up is when we discover what is true in our lives, our faith, our friends. If we can carry those truths to our highs, then there is nothing we cannot accomplish, and we will be able to see the world clearly and without fear. I raise my ice cream spoon to all the Vikings, even those who have never set foot on the trail. Here's to good friends. Here's to laughter. Here's to zero-mile days, twenty-four mile days, ice cream, new socks, cold mountain springs, the random kindness of strangers, and the power of an adventure well met. I can hear the Wolf's call: "There's more to see and do, and it's time to move on down the trail."

Pictures, maps, and more stories can be found at
www.EndtoEnding.com

LaVergne, TN USA
23 November 2010
205968LV00002B/1/P